MERE MASCULINITY

A Man's Journey to Spiritual Fitness

BARRY S. JENKINS SR.

Mere Masculinity

A Man's Journey to Spiritual Fitness

For bookings or more information, please contact:

info@BarryJenkins.org

Published by:

Latte Media Group

1030 E. Hwy. 377, Suite 110 Box 184

Granbury, TX 76048

www.LatteBros.com

Edited by:

Eric Hulet

pastoreric@gracesoamazing.org

Illustration of father and son by:

Kathy Hooper

ISBN 978-0-9988055-0-4

Printed in the United States of America.

Contents

Endorsements

The Lord's design and criteria for Kingdom rulership has been clearly communicated. In the Old Testament Book of 1 Samuel, we read that God sought "a man after His own heart" (v.14). Acts 13:22 reveals that He found His man: "I have found David son of Jesse, a man after my own heart; he will do everything I want him to do."

This significant work by Pastor Barry Jenkins will inspire men to understand, discover, and connect to God's design and purpose for their lives. Ultimately, there is no higher calling and no greater fulfillment than to become fully God's man, after His own heart. "Mere Masculinity" helps to lead the way home to such promise.

Glenn C. Burris, Jr.
President, The Foursquare Church

(Endorsements Continued)

Is there a simple answer to the question or definition of masculinity? Every man who is honest enough to admit it has struggled with what it means to be a man in at least some of the roles we are expected to fill. Statistics today reveal that far too many men grow up with no positive male role model which leaves them with even greater struggles, and a huge majority populate our prison systems.

Barry Jenkins has given personal and biblical information that will cause you to think—perhaps in ways you have never thought before regarding how to be the man you were created to be. If you are serious about making choices that will enable you to find and follow God's plan for your life as a godly man, this book can help you do that.

May the Lord bless you as you seek Him and His ways as a man.

Glenn L. Ward
Director of Missions
Paluxy Baptist Association

Dedication

It is only fitting that this book should be dedicated to the one whose living-example of faith has given me many years of inspiration. For over forty years his strength, leadership, integrity, and loving spirit have been beacons of hope lighting a clear pathway to Jesus, not only for me, but for an entire community.

In any number of situations, having asked the first question, "What would Jesus do?" The next question I would ask is, "What would Bishop do?"

His many accolades include: Mayor, Vice-Mayor, Bishop, Pastor, father, and friend.

As my Pastor, my brother, my friend, and my mentor, Bishop Henry Hearns has one title no other man has; he is my father in Christ.

Bishop, Cozzette, the kids, and I love you and appreciate you more than words could ever say.

Honorable Mention

The author would like to express his most sincere gratitude to the following people; without whose love, dedication, contribution, and faithfulness this book would not have been possible:

Cozzette Jenkins

Bishop Henry Hearns

Reverend Glenn C. Burris

Reverend Eric Hulet

Reverend Glenn Ward

Pastor Jan Spencer

Pastor Kim Pitner

Pastor Mark Fox

Pastor Robert Colwell

Thank you!

Render therefore to all their due: taxes to whom taxes are due, customs to whom customs, fear to whom fear, honor to whom honor.

(Rom 13:7)

Prelude

It was during one of those life-testing moments when I was on the road to Houston from Dallas for our denomination's Annual Conference. Troubled over some issues regarding the release of my first book, that day it just seemed pointless to continue writing.

During the four-hour drive I poured my heart out to God, letting Him know that I decided not to finish *this* book, *Mere Masculinity,* as well as other books He had inspired me to write. "I am finished writing!" I said to the Lord.

The Convention Center was filled with nearly thirty-six-hundred fellow pastors when I arrived. By the end of that evening, our keynote speaker (Jack Hayford) asked us to pray for each other in groups of five to six.

The pastors in my group were unknown to me, and I just did not feel comfortable discussing what was on my heart with strangers.

When it was my turn to share what I needed prayer for, I "passed." After all, "What further need was there of prayer?" I prayed all the way there and had made my decision.

And so, I prayed for the other pastors in my group, while concealing the matter that was weighing on my own conscience.

Several minutes later Pastor Jack dismissed us, the lights in the Convention Center came on, and most people were leaving, save a few stragglers who had slowed to catch up on old-times.

Within moments, the Convention Center was nearly empty. I was just about to head for the door myself, when one of the men from the prayer group I was in came back over and said, "The Lord told me I was not finished praying for you!"

With that he began quoting the following verses of scripture:

I write to you, little children,
because your sins are forgiven you for His name's sake.

I write to you, fathers,
because you have known Him who is from the beginning.

I write to you, young men,
because you have overcome the wicked one.

I write to you, little children,
because you have known the Father.

I have written to you, fathers,
because you have known Him who is from the beginning.

I have written to you, young men, because you are strong,
and the word of God abides in you, and you have overcome the
wicked one.
(1 John 2:12-14)

Having recited these verses in his prayer, that pastor then pointed to me and said, "The Lord said, 'You write to them now'." He then turned and walked away.

There was no question the Lord used that man to respond to my decision to quit writing. That night, from somebody I had never met before, came inarguably the voice of the Lord, bringing at once rebuke for my pity party and the encouragement I needed to press on.

It was clear that He wanted this work finished; so important was the matter to the Lord, that there came a near-instant response to the one-sided discussion I had with Him on the drive down.

By that response I understood that God had something urgent to say to men.

What follows is that message.

Introduction

What is "Manhood?"

The way a man answers that question says a lot about who he is. Yet, interestingly enough, at the time of this writing, Wikipedia had no definition, but simply redirected readers to the word, *masculinity.*

Dictionary.com, however, gave us five descriptions commonly associated with the term "Manhood:"

1. The state or time of being a man or adult male person; male maturity.
2. Traditional manly qualities.
3. Maleness, as distinguished from femaleness.
4. Virility; potency.
5. Male genitalia.

These are common definitions, but do any of them truly tell us what "manhood" is all about? What about what Manhood is *supposed to be?* More importantly, what do we need to know, if we ever hope to become *better men?*

To answer that question, we often look to the examples set by the men who have become our role models.

Yet, even our best role model and our greatest hero are not perfect. If we only follow *their* example, we will eventually run into some of the same problems they did.

So, how can we get a better understanding of manhood?

There is One Man to whom we can turn for a better understanding. His life is our example for strength, courage, and all that we can ever hope to be. His name is Jesus.

In, "Mere Masculinity," I invite you to explore this question of manhood more deeply than perhaps you ever have before.

As you read, make it personal. Ask God to speak to you.

We know God speaks to both men and women. Yet, what He has to say to men will not always be the same as what He says to women.

As you read and pray, ask God to show you what it is *He* wants you to understand uniquely. Then, be ready to make a difference, not only in your life, but also in the lives of people around you.

In the pages to follow we will go back to "The Beginning" to take a hard look at what actually happened in the Garden, and see how that affects our view of masculinity today.

If you are reading this book you are likely to be among those who feel that you have already figured that out. Whether that is you or not, there is revelation to follow that will challenge you for the better and enrich your world.

Some of the principles to follow may seem counter-intuitive; some might outright conflict with the core of your current understanding of what it means to be a man.

This book does not "sugar coat" issues that we face, and it is not intended to reinforce a world view. It is designed to help you bring life to the uniquely male covenant God has called you into.

My prayer is that men everywhere will view this message with unguarded hearts, and as a result find a biblical perspective of manhood that was not seen before; and that by so doing find deliverance, strength, and new-life.

MERE MASCULINITY

A Man's Journey to Spiritual Fitness

BARRY S. JENKINS SR.

My Awakening

But this time there was no wait. This time His word came in nearly an instant.

I t was the most difficult season of my life. The doctors could see that there was something wrong, but they were at a loss. Every waking moment was filled with pain. Relentless chills ran constantly through my body despite the intense heat of the Mojave summer.

For months I pressed on thinking that recovery was just around the corner. It was in that hope, while traveling with Cozzette to her uncle's funeral in Missouri later that year, that things took a turn.

By then it was one of the coldest days of the Missouri winter.

During that trip breathing was becoming more difficult. Most of the day I stayed alone in the hotel room waiting for time to pass so we could go home.

Days later the funeral services were over, and we headed back. Once we got to the airport, each step towards the airplane made it harder to breathe.

When we landed in Los Angeles, we got our luggage, and I collapsed on a bench just outside of the baggage claim. Struggling to inhale, I could go no further.

I had no frame of reference with which to measure how sick I had become. I thought it was just the flu. But any colds or the flu I had before, no matter how bad they were, always went away after a few days or weeks.

This time was different. Whatever this was, I had been fighting it for far too long. This time, instead of getting better, it was getting worse. And, my body showed no signs of bouncing back.

When we got home from the airport I climbed into a La-Z-Boy recliner and tried to rest. Within a few minutes Cozzette knew she had to get me to the hospital and get me there fast.

A few hours later the first diagnosis came in. It was pneumonia. But, pneumonia was not the end of it.

After administering some antibiotics and breathing treatments, the hospital sent us home.

They said that I should be "good as new" within about two weeks, but that did not happen. The antibiotics were not working, and, over the next several months, stronger antibiotics were given.

My complexion worsened as I turned pale grey and became lethargic. Whenever I could sleep I was frequently awakened by severe chills and violent coughing. For months it was difficult to eat – when I was able to eat at all.

There were no normal nights, no deep or refreshing sleep. In its place were long hours of misery, discomfort, pain, and *loneliness*.

Treatment for pneumonia went on for nearly a year. Eventually, a lung specialist diagnosed the condition as Chronic Obstructive Pulmonary Disease (COPD) and suggested that though some people are able to live with it, I should go home and "get my affairs in order."

This was no longer some spell of sickness. This was very different. I was on the edge, being neither dead nor alive. Every moment was questionable, and every breath a struggle.

Each night I laid there in desperate need of sleep. As I began to drift, I was revived by an adrenal rush spurred on by the thought that if I dozed off completely, I would stop breathing and never wake.

Days became weeks, weeks slipped into months, and months were becoming years. Hope that there would ever be a resemblance of life as I once had known it was fading.

With the passage of time I began to think that there were things I would never get to do, life I would never get to live, and dreams that

I would never see.

Right then, all of my past accomplishments seemed vain. All my cries seemed wasted breath; all I could do was surrender *completely* to God.

I was already a Christian; I had already given my life to Jesus, but this was something different. It was as though I had been asleep and was now fully awake to discover that there was something I was failing to see.

In that hour there came a letting-go; the kind that only comes with the intimate knowledge that immediately after your next breath, you may be finally and forever with the Lord.

In the brokenness of that day I had little stamina and little strength to do much of anything, that is, anything but meditate and pray.

I began to review my life. I thought about the things that were truly important, as well as grieved over the insignificant things that so much of my time had been spent on.

It was clear that my world could have been better, had I made a few different choices. With that clarity, I began to feel a burden to bring life to those around me.

There just was not going to be enough "tomorrows" to "get around to it" anymore; there just was not going to be time to get all the things done that I was destined to accomplish before I died.

Broken, dismantled, and disarmed, there was no desire to defend myself. Instead there was only a longing to be closer to God and see things *His* way.

I had gone far beyond all thoughts of, "Why me?" In its place was the humble realization of how insignificant I was, and how truly important He is.

Compounding that trial was knowing that Cozzette was also suffering. It was the silent outcry of a barren womb. It was a pain that took this man fifteen years to understand. Cozzette's pain would only be multiplied if her hopes and dreams were to perish with the death of her husband.

With my strength failing and wit gone, there seemed to be nothing I could do to comfort her.

All that remained of our lives appeared broken, shattered by the reality of that day.

We were Christians. Yet, we had no theology to explain why this was happening.

Much of the time I was too weak to even pray.

My life was prostrate before Him.

There at the crossroads of humility and surrender, right there where lifelessness lurked at death's door, at the place of my darkest hour, there came an awakening.

It was in that hour, while longing desperately for a touch from God, that the inspiration came for this book.

As a preacher, I regularly brought messages of hope and encouragement to others. I knew how to pray and wait on the Lord for what (if anything) He wanted me to say to *them*. Now it was *my* turn to pray and wait on God for myself.

My prayers were specific. They were no longer about all the material things I once thought I needed. All I wanted from God was to get my health back and live.

Right there, where all of my hopes and dreams were overshadowed by so great an infirmity, the Lord spoke clearly to me.

It was a message directed at the very framework of my impediment. It was a message destined to refine my definition of *masculinity.*

With this message God was cutting away the foreskin of my heart; revealing a word that would enable this man to understand what *God intended masculinity to be.*

Because of what God said that day, my understanding of what it means to be a man would change forever.

And, as a result of that change, neither my world nor Cozzette's would ever be the same.

My Change

I know you have faith, but right now I need you to grow.

Change needs to come whenever you realize that the road you are taking is not getting you very far. That is the place where you have a choice. You can dig in and hold on to your old ways, or you can open your heart to new direction and new possibilities.

I am not talking about salvation, although the same holds true for salvation. What I am talking about here is *Christian living*.

I am talking about what happens *after* we have taken our cares and concerns to the cross, and having done that, there still comes an overwhelming realization that we are falling short of our potential.

As Christians, by definition we are followers-of-Christ. But, even our best efforts to follow are sometimes hindered by our own limited understanding. Add to that the challenges we all face, and over time, we often build layer upon layer of viewpoints that are contrary to God.

I believe most of us can think of a time or two when we were fully persuaded that we knew what we were doing, but later, when God gave us a better insight, we discovered that we were actually in opposition to Him.

Anytime we take a position that opposes God, we limit ourselves.

Learning to Follow

Because we all start out with a limited understanding, we must accept the fact that we need His help, even in something as simple as following Him.

Sometimes God's help does not come the way we want it to. Sometimes His help comes by way of a tough lesson. Those tough lessons are often God "chipping away" at the build-up of ideas we acquired that *did not* come from Him.

The Bible tells us that the Lord chastens those He loves, and chastises every child He accepts. Knowing this, it makes sense to pay close attention to what God is telling us, especially when things get rough.

Needless to say, things got rough for me the year I got sick. Some may argue that a lack of faith caused my illness. But, I am here to tell you it was not about a lack of faith. Not everything that happens to you, not everything you are going through is because of a lack of faith.

For those of us who are bent on doing things our own way, God will use a difficult situation to humble us, so that our hearts will open to hear what He is saying.

Throughout the most difficult time, my faith was squarely in Him and had been most of my adult life. Faith was not the issue. It was one of those, "add to your faith" moments the Bible talks about in 2 Peter Chapter 1.

God showed me that day that my sickness was an outward manifestation of the way I understood manhood. If there was anything I knew, I knew what the Bible said about men and women. I had all the answers; my mind was fixed on those ideas. I didn't want to change, and didn't realize that I was no longer growing.

It was as though it took being sick for me to hear the Lord saying, "I know you have faith, but now I need you to grow."

In order for growth to happen, a heart had to be exposed, mine. Some views had to be released, again mine. And someone needed to deal with some problems. You guessed it, me.

Funny, but at the time there was not anything I saw as *my* problem.

Lesson One

Prior to that season my understanding of faith subtly led me to believe that when Jesus went to the cross, He freed me of some responsibilities. But, is that really what He came to do?

God never said that His paying the penalty for our sin and iniquities meant *we* no longer have *responsibilities.*

On the contrary. When you truly have faith, you will see the need to go beyond just the things that make life better for *you.* In short, true faith will bring you out of yourself and give you a greater sense of responsibility to *the world around you.*

I was getting it, but I was getting this lesson at a tough time. With God speaking, I began to see that there was a particular problem that for fifteen years I failed to recognize as mine — even though it had my name written all over it. It was something so simple and natural for most people, but, for me and my wife, it was just not happening. We wanted to have children.

We had been to the doctors. We knew *technically* what was wrong, but there was a deeper issue at work which could not be measured by a lab report or diagnosed by a doctor.

The problem was not simply physical; it had to do with the mindset of the man. It was the way I viewed my responsibilities as a husband.

Prior to that I thought being a good husband was about my ability to provide, my physical abilities, and about respect. I thought my first responsibility (and the responsibility of those in my care) was to *my vision,* and that my accomplishments would eventually mean success for those who helped me reach my goals.

With that old view I was very sensitive to the way people treated me.

I made sure to *draw the line* and let people know when they had gone too far. At the same time, I was not willing to go beyond any lines that I drew.

I'm not talking about simply setting boundaries. We all need to set *healthy* boundaries. What I'm talking about is setting boundaries without discussing them with God.

Before that day my boundaries were based on learned assumptions about rights, privileges, and the authority God specifically gives us as men.

Infertility was something *outside the lines.* I saw it as uniquely Cozzette's problem, God's problem, anyone's problem but mine.

Having already fathered two children, I knew there was nothing wrong with "the fellas." What God taught me in that hour was that just because my "boys" were okay, so to speak, it did not mean the problem was not with me.

It was not until becoming sick that I began to understand, confront, and deal with the whole infertility issue. But more importantly, I began to see a problem with the way many of us as men view our world.

It was the very views that I once thought would protect me and make me strong, which were, in fact, making me weak.

God showed me that masculinity has *more to do* with a man's willingness to bring life to *the world around him.* That means being strong enough to go beyond his own set boundaries. When you think about it, isn't that *exactly* what Jesus did?

In the midst of illness, barrenness and brokenness, God took the time to show me how taking responsibility is *essential* to manhood, and as I tuned in there came renewed hope.

Prior to that day I had been ill for so long that I no longer made plans, and I had stopped dreaming about the future. I was ready to give up, and the thought of dying brought a sense of relief.

But God revived me and showed me that there was not only more life for me to live, He had more life for me to *give.* As I paid close attention to what He was saying, I found myself dreaming again.

I began to see that not only was it important to God for my wife and I to have children, but God wanted to birth new life, hope, and promise in the world around us. It became perfectly clear that *that* new life, *that* hope, and *that* promise, had to be sown and cultivated by *this* man.

That lesson was like getting an urgent memo from God. While I received the message God had *specifically for me*, it also came with instructions. God wanted me to go share it.

Suddenly there was this keen awareness that my own healing, as well as the children we were wanting, were all hinged upon my response to His message on manhood and whether I was willing to be faithful with it.

Having faith means trusting in God. But being *faith-full* means that God can trust *you.*

God was showing me where I needed to be faithful.

With that there was an understanding that He was not only giving me a memo, God was giving me a *mandate*.

It was time to quit waiting for someone else to write and teach this message.

It was time to put my faith to work.

On the surface, this appeared to contradict the message of faith as I once understood it. After all, since Jesus "paid it all," salvation is no longer a matter of works, but of faith.

But the work laid before me was not a salvation-work, nor was it an attempt to earn favor with God; this was a *growth-work*. This was a "telios (perfect)" work, which is the natural response of any heart that has been born again and is maturing in Christ.

Jesus said, "I always do what is pleasing to Him." By His example, we see that doing the things that are pleasing to God *is what we are called to as men.*

So, what pleases Him?

Reflection and Discussion

1. Have you ever "stood your ground" on a subject, only to discover that you were partially, or completely wrong?

2. Has God ever taught you an important lesson through a difficult situation?

3. If so, what did you do?

4. How did that experience change the way you see your responsibilities as a man?

5. How did that lesson affect the way you understand God?

My Promise

Then he asked Jesse, "Is this it? Are there no more sons?" "Well, yes, there is the runt. But he is out tending the sheep." Samuel ordered Jesse, "Go get him. We are not moving from this spot until he is here."

Jesse sent for him. He was brought in, the very picture of health—bright-eyed, good-looking. GOD said, "Up on your feet! Anoint him! This is the one."

Samuel took his flask of oil and anointed him, with his brothers standing around watching. The Spirit of GOD entered David like a rush of wind, God vitally empowering him for the rest of his life. Samuel left and went home to Ramah.

1 Samuel 16:11-13 (MSG)

During that difficult season the Lord comforted me by reminding me of His promises—Promises that had not yet been realized.

There is power in a promise. In our promises, we have hope. In hope we find strength.

When I think about my childhood, one thing I remember is that my father always kept his promises to me. It was not a "Father Knows Best" situation by any means; we had serious issues. Yet, it was important for him to know that I trusted him to keep his word. As a child, his kept promises gave me strength.

Many years later, when I was diagnosed with lung disease, my life was as low as it had ever been. At the same time, I knew that I had promises from God that I had yet to see. With that in mind, I began to think about the many examples in the Bible where God gave someone a promise, and His promise changed that person's life.

I took a closer look at the promises God gave to David.

I thought about how God is creative. His very Word creates life. By His Word everything that was created came into existence.

When God gives you a promise, He is giving you His Word. He is giving you the same thing that made all of creation.

Knowing that, and seeing how God's promises made life better for David, encouraged me to know that His promises would make life better for me.

But, what was it about David that prompted God to promise him so much?

We are introduced to David in 1 Samuel chapter 16. During that time, Saul was the King of Israel.

It was a time when both the king and the kingdom were plagued by compromise within and enemies without.

On the surface, Saul was a mighty warrior. But on the inside, something was very wrong. Though God gave Saul clear instructions, Saul didn't take God at His word. Instead, he chose to *ignore* what God told him, and do what *he thought* was best for himself and the kingdom. He was more motivated by what the people thought than what God thought.

Even though God was with Israel and her king, and even though He had done many miraculous things through them, because of their unwillingness to follow Him, as long as Saul reigned, they would never live up to their best.

While Saul's leadership gave the people *temporary* victories, their future was dying.

If you want the promise of a better life, you have to begin by taking God at His word. When you honor what God has *already* said, you are bringing life to the promise of a better future.

God needed His people to have a leader who understood that. He knew that it just wasn't in Saul. Because it wasn't, He went looking for a new king.

God had someone specific in mind, and sent Samuel to find and anoint that person.

When he got to David's house, Samuel asked David's father Jesse to bring all his sons out, to see which one it was that God had chosen to be the next king. The "test" was that Samuel would try to pour oil from a flask on each one of Jesse's sons. If that son was *not* God's choice, the oil would not flow.

One by one, Jesse brought his sons to Samuel to see which one God would release His oil upon. Yet, the oil did not flow on any of the sons Jesse brought out.

Jesse was confused. He brought out the best that he had, and none of them passed the test. What's remarkable, is that it never even entered his mind, that his son David could be the one. Jesse never even thought to give David a try.

In the mind of his own father, David didn't have it in him to be a king. After all, as far as his family was concerned, David was good for little more than tending sheep.

Yet, God saw something in David that even his father could not see. He saw a man that would follow *His* heart. Because of David's desire to follow, God unlocked David's greatest promise.

David was not perfect, he didn't do everything right. But God worked through this seemingly insignificant and imperfect man to forge a better life, not just for David, but for an entire kingdom.

Let's look at David's promise.

I have found My servant David; with My holy oil I have anointed him, with whom My hand shall be established; also My arm shall strengthen him. The enemy shall not outwit him, nor the son of wickedness afflict him. I will beat down his foes before his face, and plague those who hate him.

But My faithfulness and My mercy shall be with him, and in My name his horn shall be exalted. Also I will set his hand over the sea, and his right hand over the rivers. He shall cry to Me, "You are my Father, My God, and the rock of my salvation." Also I will make him My firstborn, The highest of the kings of the earth.

My mercy I will keep for him forever, and My covenant shall stand firm with him. His seed also I will make to endure forever, and his throne as the days of heaven. If his sons forsake My law and do not walk in My judgments, if they break My statutes and do not keep My commandments, then I will punish their transgression with the rod, and their iniquity with stripes.

Nevertheless My loving kindness I will not utterly take from him, nor allow My faithfulness to fail. My covenant I will not break, nor alter the word that has gone out of My lips. Once I have sworn by My holiness;

"I will not lie to David: His seed shall endure forever, and his throne as the sun before Me; it shall be established forever like the moon, even like the faithful witness in the sky." Selah.

Psalms 89:20-37

Much of this promise is prophetic, and points to Jesus – Which is another part of the message. For now, let's focus on how this promise relates directly to David.

David was considered a ruddy, insignificant man by the people closest to him. If it were up to his family, he would have been tending their sheep his entire life.

But because *God's heart* was more important to David than anything else, God awakened a promise inside of David that empowered him to raise above the naysayers, and there was nothing and no one who could stop him.

Notice David's priorities after becoming king. He didn't put his career first, or even ambition for his own kingdom. David was constantly thinking about what God wanted, and he set his sights on *that.*

Because it was in his heart to put God first, David's promise was so great that it not only assured David a kingdom and lineage, it also made a pathway for God to build *His own* kingdom, the Kingdom of God.

Most of us today want to know that our lives have some meaningful purpose, that when it's all said and done, we will have made a lasting difference.

There's nothing more satisfying than knowing you have accomplished everything you were born to do, and your children will have the same opportunity.

That's exactly the kind of assurance God gave David – The satisfaction of knowing that not only his life was going to make a difference, but there would always be someone to carry on. It was the assurance of a rich, full life now, and an everlasting legacy—What more could any of us ask for?

Wrapped inside of David's promise was God saying, "Because of your willingness to do what's important to *Me,* I am going to build <u>two</u> kingdoms through you - yours <u>and</u> Mine."

Perhaps you are like David was in his early days. Perhaps the people around you cannot see the awesome things you were born to do. They have already counted you out and can't imagine that there is greatness in you. As far as they are concerned, you will never have what it takes to go higher.

Think about it. Even David's own father called him the "runt."

But, the difference between Saul and David was that it didn't matter to David what the people around him thought.

God had something greater in mind for David, something that even his own family couldn't imagine or see. *It was a promise.*

If it had not been for the promise God gave David, we would likely not even know his name. But because of His promise, David went on to build a kingdom and change the world in such a way that the term, "House of David" is still revered by God's people today.

What if you had a promise like that?

How many of us could wish today that God would rekindle David's promise in us?

Imagine God saying to you and me that He wants to build us a house. Imagine Him saying that He wants to build us a "strong" house, a house where our enemies are all dumbfounded and defeated, a house where our posterity abounds.

Imagine a promise from God so powerful, that through us, He could build His own kingdom!

My brother, that is exactly what God is saying to you and me today!

Is God finished building His kingdom?

Of course not. But the way God has chosen to build it is through the promise of David.

Since David is no longer here to do it, there remains a promise for us today, that God will continue building His kingdom through those of us who are willing to find and follow *His* heart.

God is still looking for men today who want His promises. God is still looking for men for whom He can build a house, a lasting posterity, through whom His own kingdom will *flourish*.

David's promise was not new. It goes all the way back to the promises of Abraham. All David did was unlock the potential of God's promise that was previously given to Abraham and his heirs.

David is not the period at the end of the sentence; he is an example to all of Abraham's heirs. If Jesus is your Savior, that makes *you* an heir as well. Abraham's promise is still there for you.

The Bible says it this way:

> *And if you are Christ's, then you are Abraham's seed, and heirs according to the promise.*
>
> Galatians 3:29

All it takes is for you to put God first, like David did, and God will unlock His greatest promise in you.

What possibility! What potential!

That means that the poverty you were in yesterday, you do not have to continue in—God has given you promise!

That means the things that once kept you down, can no longer keep you. God has given you promise!

That means the haters cannot stop you. God is your promise!

That means that the cycle of hurts—Even the mistakes you made can't hold you back any longer.

The enemy cannot outwit you, nor the son of wickedness afflict you! Why? Because God's arm shall strengthen you. You are a man of promise, and God is building you a house!

God wants to bless you just like He blessed David, and all He needs to do it, is for you to trust to Him—More than you trust anyone else, even yourself.

You can never lose by trusting God. On the contrary, what you gain is one of the most valuable things you can ever have, the promise of God in you!

Reflection and Discussion

1. Can you think of a promise once made to you that was either kept or never kept?

2. How did that make you feel?

3. Have you ever broken your promise to someone?

4. How do think that promise affected the other person?

5. What are some promises God made to you, that you are still looking forward to?

6. How can you start today, to be in a better position to receive God's promises?

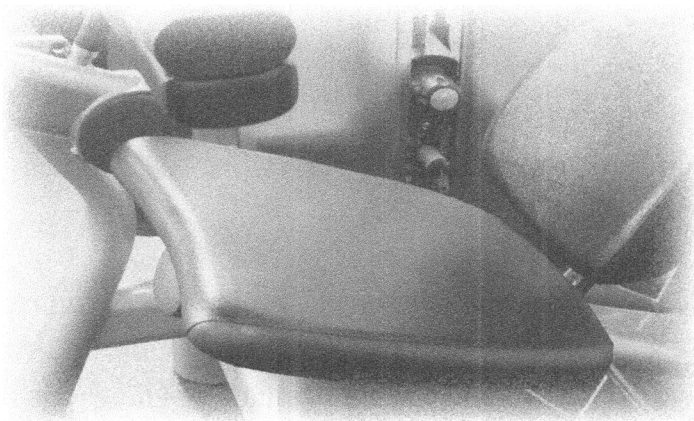

My Purpose

For surely I know the plans I have for you, says the LORD, plans for your welfare and not for harm, to give you a future with hope. Then when you call upon me and come and pray to me, I will hear you.

Jer 29:11-12 (NRSV)

In the months after that diagnosis, there came a keen awareness of all the things I had accomplished. My life was rich with blessings from God, who brought me from the ghettos of the South Bronx to places few people ever get to see. That is another story, and you can read more about it in the book, "On the Road to Glory."

The point is, it took a brush with death to make me realize that not all the things *I accomplished* fit, with that deep sense of purpose God had for me.

Have you ever gone somewhere and just known that is the place where you fit? Have you ever had a sense of purpose in being someplace or doing something? On the other hand, have you ever been someplace where there was this overwhelming feeling that you were just not supposed to be there?

When you are in the right place, somehow, someway, you know that being in *that* place, at *that* time, is exactly where God wants you. When that happens you may become mindful of how much time you spent in wrong pursuits.

> *There was a gentleman in a hospital bed covered with bandages from head to toe. Someone said to him, "What do you do for a living?"*
>
> *He said, "I'm a former window washer."*
> *Then he was asked, "When did you give it up?"*
> *The man replied, "Halfway down."*
>
> (Unknown)

Wouldn't it be great not to waste time in wrong pursuits? Wouldn't it be great to have a keen awareness that we are accomplishing the very thing for which God created us? Wouldn't it be great to be doing what we were created to do *before* we got "halfway down?"

Deep down inside we all have a unique sense of purpose. We know that somehow our purpose is connected with our destiny. That's because the purpose that *you* were born with, and that *I* was born with, are all part of God's plan.

Sometimes our *true* purpose can be difficult to understand. That is not because there is something wrong with God's plan. Our *understanding* of our purpose is connected with our willingness to go where He tells us.

"Surely I know the plans I have for you, says the LORD."

Purpose and hope, they are part of God's plan for us, and part of His plan for our world. But, no matter how hard we try, we can never find it alone; we need Him to show us the way.

In other words we have to *admit* that we can not figure it out on our own; we have to get directions. That is something, for most of us, which goes against our grain.

A Culture Shift

In the early 70's there were some changes brewing in popular music. In one top 40 song there was this strange new sound. It was different, and it worked really well.

It was the voice of an ARP Odyssey, an early synthesizer. The sound that instrument produced ushered in a revolution in music.

Back then bands were bigger. Back then it was popular to have a "Big Band" sound.

Soon after their debut, synthesizers became more sophisticated. Eventually they had the ability to imitate other instruments. As time went on synthesizers were able to play multiple instruments at the same time.

Composers today can go into the studio and single-handedly lay down all of the instrumental tracks, virtually eliminating the need for other band members.

Yet, no matter how good synthetic tracks are, no matter how well transistors *imitate* the sound of real instruments, it is never quite the same.

Artificial sound cannot truly capture the subtle nuance of human breath or the way a musician's heartbeat relates to the composition.

If you are old enough to remember pre-synthetic music, you are likely to say that there is something missing from pop music today.

It is not simply a matter of new and old, young vs. aged; it is a matter of *symphony* versus *soloist.*

Music was once a cooperative talent. It was a rhythm that brought the hearts of performers together; and it had a unique effect on the hearts and souls of its listeners.

There was a kind of fulfillment in that. It was different than what you get from a solo rhyme or clever tune. It brought listeners deeper, in a way that no single synthetic melody can do.

Drum Beats

As for me, I always loved the drums. Some of my earliest memories are of my dad playing congas with his old army buddies. Their music inspired me.

By elementary school I had my first drum set and was studying at the famed Bronx House Music School.

While many kids in junior high were going out for sports, I was playing professionally for groups like Jimmy Dockett's Love Unlimited Orchestra (Flo-Feel Records) and the Michael Hill's Blues Mob.

After high school, like most musicians I still needed a day job. That is the job that pays the bills while waiting to get your musical career off the ground. So, by the early 80's I had moved from New York to Los Angeles to work in the aerospace industry.

As far as music was concerned, it was tough getting re-established after that move.

Working full-time by day, I did some recording for various producers whenever the opportunity came.

One day I met a composer who was trying to break into the music business. We seemed to get along, and he asked me to join him in the studio to do some recording.

We rehearsed for several days. After that we loaded up in his van to go make a record.

Upon our arrival, the owner of the studio seemed to know this composer very well. "Who is the drummer?" He asked. When my friend introduced me, the studio's owner refused to look me in the eye.

As I set up the drums, there was a strong sense that this man did not want me there. It was as though he viewed me as a competitor, but there were no other drums around.

As we began to play there were funny sounds in my headset. It was another beat, and it was not coming from me. That strange beat was not at all in sync with the music.

"See, I told you that drummer was not going to work out," he told the composer. That guy did not know me, nor had he ever heard me play before.

Unknown to me, that guy had a new toy. He had a drum machine, and he was trying to convince the composer that there was no need to record with real drummers anymore.

To prove his point, he was sabotaging the drum tracks. He was piping in erroneous beats while I was playing. Of course the composer could not tell the difference between what I was playing, and what was coming from the drum machine.

After just a few minutes I was asked to sit out the session, while the two of them went on to lay down every track, from guitars, drums and bass, to horns and keys.

Though the finished music sounded much like a nine-piece band, it was just the two of them, nothing more.

Today you can buy synthesizers with thousands of voices, including synthesizers with drum machines and sequencers built in.

You can do some really great things; you can make some really cool music all by yourself, but there will always be something missing.

You cannot synthesize the passion another human brings to the composition.

Pre-solo-synthetic music required people working together; breathing together in such a way that their combined talents produced more than notes.

Regardless of how well it imitates the original, solo-synthetic music is missing that element; it does not have the breath of multiple human beings, it does not come from the hearts of people working together.

Today many artists have a "solo" perspective. To them it is not about *us* making melody; it is about *me and my music.*

Yes, there are still bands that use the synthesizer as *one* of the instruments in their tool-box; but if you listen to pop music today, it is becoming harder to find them.

Not Just in the Music

During that same era, while the music was changing, many corporations were downsizing. Factories around the world were shutting down, making way for robotics. Countless jobs were eliminated.

More and more we are living in a multi-tasking world where things that once took many people to do, can now be done by a single person.

Technology in and of itself is not the problem. Having said that, with the application of today's technologies, more and more venues are becoming monotone; they are becoming synthetic.

We no longer need secretaries, we have smart phones and voicemail systems. We do not even have to leave our homes to go shopping or to do our banking. There is so much that comes to us, without our ever having to deal with others.

Solo, it is not just a musical term anymore. It is fast becoming the mantra of our culture.

We no longer need to interact with as many people in our day-to-day lives.

There was a time when the church and the town square were the social mecca of the community.

We now live in an ever increasing virtual world, a world where we do not have to look in someone's eyes when we are doing business with them.

Today, we rely heavily on social media; with it we can accomplish some great things. People are finding lost friends, they are connecting across vast distances. Yet for all social media has done for us, there is something missing.

When I am face-to-face with you, if there is something on your heart, I can feel it.

Online you cannot feel people. You cannot see how their breath changes in response to their circumstance.

Today we have more freedom than ever. We are free to be alone, free to create a world that revolves purely around *our individuality.*

While that may feel nice, where is God in all that?

Let's face it, there are times when going solo is appropriate; there are times when one lone voice can become a beacon to shine the way.

Having said that, the pendulum has shifted in such a way that we are not necessarily a lone voice above the crowd, but are becoming isolated voices of increasingly lesser significance.

I Need What?

When Cozzette and I started our computer business many years ago, we did what many people do. We looked at all the jobs it took to run a business, and we reasoned, "I can do that."

Perhaps the biggest lesson we learned from that experience is that while there *are* things you can do alone, there are also things that should be left to others. We learned that bringing people together, and letting each of them contribute their own unique talents is what truly makes a business great.

Today it is no longer about music; it is not just about business. There is a cadence; a crescendo coming from a culture that is humming, "I do not need you."

With that, the same downsizing that began in our music and in our industry is now happening in our *relationships*.

If you hurt me, I do not need you. If you do not do what I say, I do not need you. If you do not agree with me, I do not need you.

People seem to lack the heart it takes to go the distance anymore.

They are not committed for the long haul. People want their way wholly and completely, and they want it right now.

The moment tough times come, there is no shortage of counselors; of broken people waiting in the wings to whisper in your ear, "You do not need anybody... You can do it by yourself."

That may sound noble. Kicking people to the curb may make you feel strong in the *short term*. But in the long run, it does not make you stronger, it makes you *weaker*.

There may be times when God calls you to separate yourself; Abraham is an example. Yet, even Abraham took his direction from God, not from broken counselors.

Why is this important? And, what does this have to do with our purpose?

His Body

God has created us in such a way that we <u>absolutely need each other.</u> We were made to interdependently learn, grow, love, and derive a sense of purpose.

Let's look at one of the fundamental wonders given to us by God.

When boy-meets-girl and the sparks fly, a bond is formed. When they marry, the two become one.

He is fulfilled when he releases life. Her joy is made complete as she receives life from him. God is glorified in the conception.

Relationships are a symphony. They are an example to us that life is supposed to include other people; we need each other.

Closer to home
When my wife and I were trying to have children, we saw a number of doctors. With each new doctor we went to, the questions started out the same; they asked if we "crescendo" together.

The doctors could not explain why, but they knew that when a couple reaches their peak at the same time they were more likely to have a valid pregnancy. In other words, we are more likely to have children when we are in sync.

His Example
God could have chosen to be by Himself; to be without us. Yes, He could have chosen to make a synthetic world.

He certainly does not *need* us, yet He chose to create us and share His life and His world *with us.*

I know a few guys who do well in the spotlight. Yet for some reason one-on-one they are very cold-hearted and cannot seem to get close to anybody.

These guys are very controlling. Everything has to be exactly the way *they* see it. Their wives can never measure up, and consequently they do not stay married long.

How many divorces does it take to reach your goals? How many times do you have to fail before you realize you cannot do it alone?

Christians are not exempt from this.

True spirituality is not synthetic, antiseptic, or singular. If it is only self-fulfilling, it is <u>not</u> God's purpose.

In the 10th chapter of Luke's gospel we find examples of religious leaders who were more concerned with themselves than with the people they were called to serve.

"A certain man fell among thieves," Jesus said, but the priest and the Levite were too busy. . .

Maybe they had to get the sanctuary ready for service. Maybe they had to attend a luncheon, or maybe they had to head up a men's group.

In the 12th chapter of Mark's gospel some Sadducees came to Jesus, "Teacher, the Law says, that if a man dies . . ."

They knew the words, they quoted them to Jesus. But He simply answered,

> . . . *Are you not therefore mistaken, because you do not know the Scriptures nor the power of God?*
>
> Mark 12:24

These were people, who, though they could quote scripture verbatim, their understanding and application only went as far as to reinforce their own self-centeredness.

My brother, we have to come out of ourselves.

Our greatest life comes when we gain a sense of purpose that goes beyond any one of us individually.

Our true and God-given purpose cannot be masked by either religious rhetoric or busywork.

So what is God's purpose for you?

The simple answer to that question is that His purpose for you is as individual as you are.

Having said that, if our sense of purpose does not include helping others reach *their* purpose, our world will suffer; and, in that neglect *we* fall short of our own true purpose.

But, when I see my purpose in terms of unlocking the potential in the people around me, then what I have is mutually fulfilling and ultimately more gratifying.

Be honest with yourself. How do you view the people in your world? Are they in your life just for your own fulfillment? Is it all about you?

Have you decided that once you make it, whatever *they* need should "trickle down" to them? Or, do you view the people in your world in terms of *your responsibility to help them?* Clearly the latter is the biblical view.

There is power in a symphony. There is strength in a concerted breath.

Our grander purpose is to fit "jointly" together, so that *together* we animate God's church.

When we do that, we discover that what we have is far richer than anything the solo-synthetic can offer.

It is important to God that we learn to play nice, *together.*

It is not all about any one of us.

> *I want you to think about how all this makes you more significant, not less. A body isn't just a single part blown up into something huge. It is all the different-but-similar parts arranged and functioning together.*
>
> 1 Corinthians 12:14 (MSG)

You cannot fake this... You cannot isolate your part of the body; you cannot find your purpose without being *connected.*

Finding your purpose means rejecting the natural tendencies we have to go it alone.

It takes becoming a man after God's own heart. It is while in the pursuit of *His heart* that we find our greatest potential.

Truly there is no greater platform from which to launch a quest for purpose than a heart completely yielded to the will of God.

Regardless of your purpose *uniquely;* all of us, as men, have a common purpose, that is to follow the heart of God and cultivate life in the world around us.

When we come to that realization, there comes an overwhelming sense that we are right where we need to be.

Suddenly we fit. We are hearing from the Lord, and our God-given purpose takes on new life.

Reflection and Discussion

1. Have you ever considered that your purpose may be part of a combined purpose, where you work together as a group?

2. Are there any ways you can think of, where joining together with people having a common purpose can reach a greater purpose together for God?

3. Have you found your God-given purpose?

4. How do you know?

*T*here is a great old Church Hymn "Come Thy Fount of Every Blessing." In the third stanza of this hymn the words of the heart come forth;

'Bind my wandering heart to Thee, prone to wander, Lord, I feel it, prone to leave the God I love; here's my heart, O take and seal it, seal it for Thy courts above'

Our hearts have the human tendency to wander from the courts of the love of God. When we wander we start following paths that make us dull of hearing as to what His heart truly is saying to us.

The ability to receive His heart as we read the word of God comes from meekness; it comes from the place where the heart is completely surrendered to Him. We have a responsibility to surrender our hearts to Him, and seal them there.

The sealed heart requires seeking; the turning of affection from lower things to the higher courts of our Lord. This will produce the true heart of the man God called us to be; the man who operates from the rich eternal treasures only found in the sealed heart of Christ!

Pastor Mark Fox
The Way to Jerusalem Church
Wellston, OK

My Heart

*And Samuel said to Saul, "You have done foolishly. You have not kept the commandment of the LORD your God, which He commanded you. For now the LORD would have established your kingdom over Israel forever. But now your kingdom shall not continue. **The LORD has sought for Himself a man after His own heart, and the LORD has commanded him to be commander over His people,** because you have not kept what the LORD commanded you."*

1 Sam 13:13-14

Who has not, at some time or another been faced with a major decision, and in the process of sorting it out someone says, "Just follow your heart."?

But, is that sound advice? Or better yet, *should* you trust your heart?

I do not know about you, but I have done that from time to time. . . Just followed my heart. I have probably done that more often than I care to admit.

However, the closer I draw to the Lord, the more I understand *my* heart is not perfect, and when I trust in what is *not* perfect, the decisions I make are also less than perfect.

Not all decisions that favor the heart are flawed. For example, my decision to marry Cozzette, as it turns out, was a good one. But even though I got what my heart wanted, I allowed the Lord to weigh-in on that decision.

What I am saying is that when we make decisions, and those decisions are based *exclusively* on the counsel of our own hearts, the outcome is typically not what we expect and seldom what we want.

Over the process of time I have come to understand that my heart does not always know what's best for me.

One of the reasons for that is that my heart speaks to me through feelings.

Feelings change from day to day. A decision made today that is based on a feeling will not mean the same thing to me when those feelings change.

I realized that if I am going to have a better life, I have to make better choices. And, if I am going to make better choices, I have to find something better to base my decisions on than my own fickle feeble heart.

I do not know about you, but I am hoping that tomorrow is going to be better than yesterday. I am looking to *grow*.

Let's see what the Bible has to say about growth and heart. . .

> *Blessed is the man who trusts in the LORD, and whose hope is the LORD.*
>
> *For he shall be like a tree planted by the waters, which spreads out its roots by the river, and will not fear when heat comes; but its leaf will be green, and will not be anxious in the year of drought, nor will cease from yielding fruit.*
>
> *The heart is deceitful above all things, and desperately wicked; who can know it?*
>
> Jer 17:7-9

We can see here that we prosper when we shift our trust from our own, what the Bible calls, "wicked" hearts.

The bottom line is that if we want to live better, we have to stop relying on our feelings; we have to learn to hear and follow *Him*.

The question now becomes, "How do we do that?" How can we be sure, when making decisions, that we are following the Lord's heart rather than our own?

In the months following my diagnosis, I began to think about that question, and the Lord spoke clearly to me. I understood Him telling me to *search for His heart in* **every** *situation.*

With *that* understanding I began a study of the Bible from a different perspective. It was no longer about reading for what *I wanted* to get out of it. It became critically important to find God's heart in every chapter and verse.

Today my goal is to live each moment mindful of that question, "Where is God's heart?" And, "What is He saying to me right now?" Simply taking the time to acknowledge God and seek His heart keeps me closer to Him and makes my priorities clear.

Interestingly enough, what God has to say when I do that is *not* what I would conclude naturally and seldom what is popular.

Heart to Heart

God has given us examples of people who sought His heart and people who did not. We can see clearly in His examples what happens to those who trust in their own hearts (or the hearts of other people), as opposed to those who live to follow the heart of God.

Two prominent examples are first Jesus, who *always* did the will of His Father, and our other example is David.

With that in mind, let's take a closer look at David, who, though he started out no different than you and I, forged a better life for himself and the people around him.

Looking back at David's day, we can see this heart issue from both sides of the aisle. It was illustrated by two kings; one king who had the heart of the people (Saul), and the other who had a heart after God (David).

What's important to note is that while Saul *managed* to become king, no power on Earth could keep him on the throne. That is because Saul refused to put God's heart *first.*

When it comes to heart, there is a sharp contrast between these kings. When he spoke to the people, Saul referred to God as *"your* God," while David referred to Him as *"my* God."

A fundamental difference between Saul and David was that Saul was a people pleaser, while David sought to please God.

Not having his heart right with God caused the first king to lose his inheritance, his posterity, and to have his kingdom ripped away; while the second heart caused its king to inherit an enduring kingdom and much more.

> *And when He had removed him (Saul), he raised up unto them David to be their king; to whom also He gave testimony, and said, I have found David the son of Jesse, a man after mine own heart, which shall fulfil all My will. Of this man's seed hath God according to his promise raised unto Israel a Saviour, Jesus.*
> Acts 13:22-23 (KJV)

Ordinary Man - Extraordinary Heart

David was a man, an ordinary man, who faced many of the same issues in life as the rest of us.

Yet, there was something about David's character that *attracted* God's favor.

There was something about the heart of this man David, that so moved God, that He took the time to let the rest of us know, *"I've found in David a man after My own heart."*

Not that David had fewer problems than the rest of us. Not that David was flawless – He made his share of mistakes.

If David were with us today, his crime would have likely had him incarcerated for life, or perhaps even sentenced to death row.

Yet, with all of his shortfalls, there was something about David that touched God's heart.

As a result, David's legacy became something that would be remembered for all time. His house became symbolic of the blessings of God.

Many generations later, even the Savior Himself was referred to as the "Son of David."

Today many people still associate godliness with the House of David.

Listen, God already told us that *our* hearts are wicked—they cannot be trusted. Yet, God was so moved by David's heart that He brought us His own kingdom, the Kingdom of God, *through* David.

The reason God could do that is that David truly allowed God to reign on the throne of his heart, to rule over it, and to be *his Lord.*

Giving God <u>full</u> authority over our hearts causes a full release of our potential, *and* creates a pathway to God's kingdom for others.

If ever there was a mortal man who lived up to his potential, it was David. His posterity and his reputation are unlike anything in history. The House of David has withstood the test of time.

Think about that for a moment. Our lives are just a brief moment in the span of time. Wouldn't it be great to know that the things we build here will endure long after we are gone?

The good news today is that all it takes to accomplish something true and lasting is to have a heart-shift!

Perhaps you never thought of that before. Perhaps you haven't given thought to the importance of keeping your Father's heart near to you.

Shortly after my eighteenth birthday I was preparing to leave home in New York and take a job in Los Angeles. Suffice it to say that it was a season when my dad and I were not communicating very well.

Nevertheless, he let me know how upset he was that I was moving so far from home. I asked dad pointedly why the thought of my leaving made him so upset. What he said was something that was a little difficult for me to understand at the time. He said, "When you get into trouble, I won't be able to reach you."

Now I am not implying that as adults we should live with or near to our parents. This is merely an illustration of one father's desire to keep his children close enough to be there through difficult times.

My father had "been there, done that." His age and experience gave him a frame of reference that I did not have. From *that* vantage point he could see the pitfalls ahead of me, and he wanted to be there to help me. He wanted me to be near enough to him so that he could reach me when I needed him.

But, there was a lot more going on, and I was ready to make my own way.

It did not take long being on my own before I learned that going it alone was the most difficult way to do things. Soon I was calling Dad just to hear his voice.

Years passed, and because of the distance, we only saw each other on a few deliberate occasions. When I got the news of his cancer, I wished I had spent more time with Dad. I wished we had been closer.

He Already Knows

As a Loving Father, God understands that there are decisions we make, things we do, which lead us into places of hurt, places of despair, places where it may be difficult to find Him. Yet, His desire is to bring us near... Close to His safety... Near to His strength.

Though God is omnipresent, there are any number of places *we* can go, situations we find ourselves in, which distance us from Him.

Pride is one of those places. Pride pushes His heart away. When we think too highly of ourselves, when we try to go it alone, we lose sight of Him.

But He gives more grace. Therefore He says: 'God resists the proud, but gives grace to the humble.'

James 4:6

Not only do we see here that pride is a *resister* to God, but, look what else is true: God "gives grace to the humble."

Humility enables us to come nearer to the source of all power. That is where we get the full measure of His grace. In other words, God's heart is our power source, and our humility keeps us *connected*.

A Humble Heart

If you study the life of David, you'll notice three things about his character:

- David was a humble man.
- He took responsibility for his world.
- He was a worshiper.

If David were here today, I believe that he would be the first one at church on Sunday and the last one to leave. David valued his relationship with the Lord. He understood that a healthy regiment of faithfulness *included* regular attendance at worship services.

There is a level of closeness we can only reach with God by coming before His throne routinely in both personal and corporate worship.

I Know All About You

Have you ever met someone for the first time, and right away that person assumed they knew all about you? I can think of a couple of times that has happened to me. I can also think of a couple of times I *wrongly* did that to someone else.

The point is, if you truly want to know a person and what's important to *them*, you cannot make assumptions. You have got to spend time with that person.

Whenever you skip the getting to know you part and jump straight to conclusions, more than likely you have misjudged that person.

There is an old saying, "You cannot judge a book by its cover."

If that is true with anything, it is even truer with God.

Every once in a while when I talk to someone about Him they say, "I am a good person," or "God knows my heart." Yes, God knows all of our hearts, that is not the issue. The question is, "How well do we know *His?*"

Sometimes people do not want their view of God to change. They may have come away from hurts with thoughts of who they think God *should be* without ever spending time with Him.

As a result they rely on how they *feel* and what they have been through.

My friends it is foolish to use *your own* life as a yardstick with which to measure God.

There is a vast difference between Him and us. His heart is pure. Our hearts are not.

Think about it for a moment. If it were possible for *you* to create a world, what would that world look like? Better yet, would people who hurt *you* ever have a future in your world?

God's heart, on the other hand, wants us to live up to our full promise; *in spite of* the fact that all of us have offended Him and even rejected Him at one time or another.

Each of us has a choice. We can continue to follow our own broken-hearts or we can reach for the integrity and purity of His.

The great news is, when we put His heart *first,* our own hearts begin to heal.

A Learning King

David did not rely on his own cunning, he inquired of the Lord. He didn't always get it right, he made mistakes—just like the rest of us. Even so, we can see that his *greatest desire* was to get it right with God.

Imagine the life-and-death decisions David had to make as king. With every decision he was subject to the same feelings we have when we make tough decisions.

Regardless of how he felt, David took time to ask, "Lord, what do *You want me to do?*" He put God above his own feelings. It takes a real man to do that! But look at the results:

> *Now therefore, thus shall you say to My servant David, "Thus says the LORD of hosts: 'I took you from the sheepfold, from following the sheep, to be ruler over My people, over Israel. And I have been with you wherever you have gone, and have cut off all your enemies from before you, and have made you a great*

name, like the name of the great men who are on the earth.

Moreover I will appoint a place for My people Israel, and will plant them, that they may dwell in a place of their own and move no more; nor shall the sons of wickedness oppress them anymore, as previously, since the time that I commanded judges to be over My people Israel, and have caused you to rest from all your enemies. Also the LORD tells you that He will make you a house.'

'When your days are fulfilled and you rest with your fathers, I will set up your seed after you, who will come from your body, and I will establish His kingdom. He shall build a house for My name, and I will establish the throne of His kingdom forever.'"

2 Sam 7:8-13

David's heart was not split between God and the things of this world.

It is no wonder God gave the promises He did to David; he knew where God lives and went there to wait for God to instruct him.

But You are holy, Enthroned in the praises of Israel.

Psa 22:3

Maybe you never considered giving your *whole* heart to God before.

Maybe you have given Him your heart in the past, but today you are just going through the motions.

Whether you have just come to know the Lord, or you have spent your entire life in ministry, it is *essential* to take a personal inventory from time to time in order to ensure that there has not come a heart-shift away from His Majesty's throne.

Right Motives - Wrong Direction

When Paul began his ministerial career he *thought* he was doing it right, and he served with all of his heart. But, even while giving God his best, he was working in absolute opposition to God.

In Acts 26:12 Paul said, "While thus occupied . . ."

It was while he was going the wrong way that Paul had a true encounter with the Living God. His life was forever changed, and he at last found the heart of God.

It does not matter what you have spent your life doing. It does not matter how many hours you spent doing what felt right.

What matters is to find God's heart right here and right now. All it takes is to admit that your heart has led you wrong. Look beyond what *your* heart is saying and listen to *His.*

It takes being humble enough to pray and admit to Him that you need His direction every hour, every minute.

That is the kind of man David was. Even at the height of his kingdom, he humbled himself and inquired of God.

What about us today? When *our* autopilot is set, will we allow God to take control? Will we let His breath fill our sails? Will we allow Him to even change our minds?

A man after God's heart understands that <u>all</u> authority comes from God. He considers that keeping his heart right with God is the most important thing he can do.

He keeps his pride in check and admits when he is wrong. He treasures the word of God, he is a worshipper, and he takes constant inventory of his own heart to know whether or not it is following God.

> *Trust in the LORD with all your heart, and lean not on your own understanding; in all your ways acknowledge Him, And He shall direct your paths.*

Prov 3:5-6

Reflection and Discussion

1. Considering this reading, have you given your "whole heart" to Jesus?

2. When was the last time you took inventory of your heart, to see if God's heart is what you are still after?

3. Do you "act first" then ask God to bless it? Or, do you pray first, and allow God to weigh in, on whether it's something you should do?

My Posterity

Most men will proclaim each his own goodness, but who can find a faithful man? The righteous man walks in his integrity; His children are blessed after him.

Prov 20:6-7

In the scriptural record we find men whose rebellion against God brought either hindrance or death to not only themselves, but also to their *posterity*. These were self-willed, high-spirited men, who refused to obey God, and eventually led His people astray.

On the other hand we find men whose deeds brought blessings for themselves, the people around them, and even the land they lived in. These are the men who sought after God, men who maintained their integrity, men who put God *first*.

Understanding Posterity

God is not standing by with a lightning bolt ready to strike any of us down for the sins of our fathers. Yet we know our father's lifestyle can have a great impact on us, and the life *we live* will affect our children.

Even before its publication, the material in this book has been life-changing for many men. Yet, because this subject matter deals with issues that skirt the boundary between Law and grace, it is necessary to clarify a few things up front, so that we can be on the same page going forward.

What comes to mind when you hear the word "sin"?

One man said that sin is an Old Testament thing; that the entire concept of sin is nullified by the New Testament. Well, that *almost* sounds right, but is sin a concept we are supposed to ignore today? The short answer is, "No."

Let's look at two verses of scripture.

> *If we confess our sins, He is faithful and just to forgive us our sins and to cleanse us from all unrighteousness. If we say that we have not sinned, we make Him a liar, and His word is not in us.*

> 1 John 1:9-10

Do not be deceived, God is not mocked; for whatever a man sows, that he will also reap.

Gal 6:7

John tells us that forgiveness from sin is *conditional,* in order to have forgiveness, we have to *admit* we have sinned.

When we turn the page from the Old Testament to the New Testament, sin does not just go away. What happens is that we are given the option, whether or not to accept a *new* accounting system. This new system (or contract) can only be entered into by faith.

Through faith in Jesus, the ledger entry that once kept score of our sin is blotted out, and in its place the new entry simply says, "See Jesus."

Of course I'm speaking figuratively. But in the Book of Romans, Chapter 4, Paul makes reference to Abraham's faith. As he does this, he uses the word "imputed" three times then once again in chapter five.

*For until the law sin was in the world, but sin is not **imputed** when there is no law.*

Rom 5:13

If you are not careful, you might read this verse to say that sin itself is no longer in existence. But, that is not exactly what the scripture is saying.

That word *imputed* is the Greek word, *ellogo.* It has to do with *accounting*—In the same sense that a storekeeper keeps an accounting of his inventory; of what is good, and what has gone bad.

When referring to the "Father of Faith" James said,

> *And the Scripture was fulfilled which says, "Abraham believed God, and it was **accounted** to him for righteousness." And he was called the friend of God.*
>
> James 2:23

The scripture is clear. It is not that sin has become some *obsolete* concept by virtue of the New Testament. What happens is that, in Christ, God makes a change to the ledger.

For those of us who, by faith, hang our hope on Jesus, God no longer *imputes* the penalty—that price is counted as being "paid in full" because of what Jesus did for us at Calvary.

Does that mean that there are no longer consequences for what we do? Certainly not. God's grace is not an open license for ungodliness— nor *unfruitfulness.*

Yes, God's grace covers a multitude of sins. Yet, at the same time, Jesus cautions us to be *fruitful.*

In Matthew 21 Jesus cursed a fig tree. That tree did not do anything wrong. It committed no sin. It was simply not doing what it was born to do—it had no fruit to offer its creator.

In Luke 19 He judged the unprofitable servant for burying his talent. We could discuss each of these passages in greater detail, however, the point here is that the law of sowing and reaping has not been repealed by the New Testament.

With that in mind, we have these two concepts, which, on the surface appear to contradict each other. The former says that we can have forgiveness of sins, while the latter reminds us that we reap what we sow.

Both of these concepts are *New Testament* concepts, and both are true. And, the way they are at once true is by the application of *grace.*

It was never God's intent to do away with the natural order of sowing and reaping. On the contrary, *through* Christ God provides *grace* to bridge the gap, when our best efforts fall short.

In 1 John 2, John tells us,

> *I write this, dear children, to guide you out of sin. But if anyone does sin, we have a Priest-Friend in the presence of the Father: Jesus Christ, righteous Jesus.*
>
> 1 John 2:1 (MSG)

My brother, we are not saved *by* good works, but we are saved *for* good works (Eph 2:10). God wants us to be *re-productive.* He does good works, and He wants us to follow in His example.

Generationally Speaking

There has been a lot of talk in recent years about "generational curses," what about that?

Well, no sin or generational curse can survive the cleansing power of Jesus. Under His system, you are made clean, and any penalty you earned is counted as being nailed to the cross with Jesus.

At the same time we know there *are* rewards for faith and hard work, both for here and in the hereafter.

What does all this have to do with posterity?

The Psalmist tells us,

> *The face of the LORD is against those who do evil, to cut off the remembrance of them from the earth.*
>
> Psa 34:16

Please take care, as we continue, not to look backwards; not to lay any blame on your fathers. To do that would be unprofitable.

Rather, gain a better understanding of how *you* impact those who come after you; those who come *through* you.

Posterity is not something we often think about. Yet, it is something that is important to God.

In Genesis 32:28, God changed Jacob's name to Israel. In subsequent reading we have to look closely to know whether God is talking to Israel the man, or Israel, the man's descendants.

A careful read through scripture shows us that God often considers us in view of our posterity. In as much as there are occasions where men *are* held accountable for the actions of their fathers, it is important to understand how God sees the man *as he relates to* his lineage.

Let's begin by looking at a man who was careful to preserve his father's posterity.

In Genesis 45 we read

> *And God sent me (Joseph) before you to preserve you a posterity in the earth, and to save your lives by a great deliverance.*
>
> Gen 45:7

If we back up just a little we find that Joseph was sold into slavery by his brothers because they were jealous of him.

Years passed. While enslaved, Joseph was falsely accused and then imprisoned. Even though his brothers' actions *initially* cost Joseph his freedom, he rose to become one of the most powerful, prominent, and influential people in the land.

But that is not the end of Joseph's story. Eventually, he came face to face with his brothers, the very ones who sold him into slavery.

Of all the things he could have said or done to them, this was a moment he must have thought about for years.

Joseph could have easily had his brothers imprisoned for what they did to him. But, instead of reading them the riot-act, instead of taking vengeance, Joseph told them how *God used* that situation to preserve *their* posterity.

By his deeds and his conversation, we can see that Joseph recognized his father's posterity as the bigger picture. That meant looking out for his brothers, even though they meant him harm.

His brothers called him a "dreamer." But Joseph was a man who knew how to hear from God. He maintained his integrity in the face of great pain, trial, temptation, and consequence; Joseph understood his *purpose*.

He could have been content with knowing that the Lord saved *him* in Egypt. He could have stopped there, and figured he had gone far enough. But he did not do that. Instead Joseph used his influence to *rescue* rather than retaliate against his brothers; and in so doing he saved *the entire lineage of Israel.*

Posterity Up Close

In Genesis 45:7 the word "posterity" comes from the Hebrew word *she'eriyth*; which refers to the remainder, the residual. Another way to say this is *descendants.*

Let's look a little closer to find God's heart in all of this.

When the Law was given, we were told clearly:

> *Fathers shall <u>not</u> be put to death for their children, nor shall the children be put to death for their fathers; a person shall be put to death for his own sin.*
>
> Deu 24:16

It is important to note that while we were given this law, at the same time we can see throughout scripture how the actions of fathers brought either devastation or deliverance to their children. How can that be?

Simply, the Law was given to *us.* In this passage we are *expressly prohibited* from putting to death either fathers or sons for each other's sins. As far as *we* are concerned, it is not *our business* to condemn anybody for what someone else did.

God wants us to understand *our* responsibilities. At the same time He alone reserves for Himself the right to exact any judgment upon both the man and his descendants.

The Heart of the Matter

Why is this so important?

To answer this question, I need to talk a little more of what I began to share with you in the opening chapters of this book.

Having been diagnosed with lung disease, one doctor said that it was "just a matter of time." He wouldn't say exactly how much time he thought I had left, but suggested I, "Go home and get my affairs in order."

There are not words to describe what went through my mind while he was speaking. I had been sick before, but had always recovered.

Time seemed to stand still that day. In that hour when time stood still, the Lord spoke to me.

The subject of His message was not new. It is one that has been studied and taught in colleges, universities, ministries, and churches throughout history. Yet, He was showing me something I had never noticed before. Something that is so clear, yet so hard to see.

As I lay on the sofa that evening, too sick to climb the stairs to the bedroom, as the weight of my illness pressed upon my chest, I began to lament with thoughts of all the dreams and plans I had that might never be realized.

At first, what the Lord said that night did not seem to make sense. Why would God choose *that particular moment* to bring such a heavy message? His message *appeared* to conflict with certain fundamentals with which I had long since come to terms.

I had investigated this subject, querying both theologians and noted clergy. What I concluded had become part of the bedrock of my understanding.

But now there I was, clinging to life, hoping for a touch from God, praying for some revelation that would begin the healing process.

"Jesus... What am I missing?" "Is there an herb or medicine I need to take?" "Is there a doctor I have not seen?" "Even so, Lord, just say the word, and I will be healed!"

God's reply was so far from what I expected. What I clearly understood Him saying that day was that my view of *manhood* was not the same as His.

Hmm...

I had been raised to understand that men and women were totally equal. But, that night there came a keen awareness that our Creator has in fact endowed us with differences *beyond* our genitalia.

Weakened from illness and distressed by the doctor's report, it felt like I was in limbo between this life and the next. And when I cried out to God with all the breath left in me, His reply began with this very verse:

> *Even Levi, who receives tithes, paid tithes through Abraham, so to speak, for he was still in the loins of his father when Melchizedek met him."*

Heb 7:9-10

At first I did not get it, so I read it again. I still did not get it, so I read it again and again.

After re-reading this verse many times that night, the lights began to come on, and the dots began to connect.

A Godly View of Posterity

In this verse, Levi is credited with paying tithes to Melchizedek through Abraham, though neither Levi, nor his father Jacob (Israel), or even *his* father Isaac, had yet been born when Abraham met Melchizedek and paid tithes to him.

That night I began to understand that God was speaking to me about the connection between *manhood* and *posterity.*

The Back Story

Before that day Cozzette and I had been married for fifteen years and had been unable to have children.

Conception problems can be challenging for any couple. When the doctor told me I had lung disease, that prognosis appeared to cast a shadow over any hope of us ever having children together.

But what really happened was that after fifteen years of barrenness, the God of Hope was going right to the core of the problem. He was revising my *theology.*

I sat there that evening, broken, vulnerable, and *available.* For once I was not *telling God* what manhood was, *I was listening.* In the quietness of that hour the Lord began to ask me some questions.

"So," He asked, "Who sinned in the garden?"

You have to understand, that in order for my former theology to work, I accepted that Eve was the bad guy, so to speak, and that Adam's sin was that he failed in his responsibility *over* his wife.

While I was about to give my response, **"Who sinned in the garden?"** The Lord asked again. This time I was a little more careful about how I would answer. This time I had to reconcile my answer against the whole of scripture. This time I had to answer, as though face to face with my Maker.

Both Adam and Eve were in the Garden. Both took and ate of the forbidden fruit. Both hid themselves when God showed up.

Yet, we are told <u>clearly</u> (Romans 5:12) that "one man's" sin brought death into the world. The article is singular, "one man." It is not referring to mankind, not referring to Eve, but to Adam *alone.*

Yes, Eve ate *first,* but we often do not consider the fact that Adam ate *as well.* In eating the forbidden fruit, both sinned the same way. Still there was something so different about Adam's sin that it condemned the rest of us.

Let's take a closer look and see what that was.

In the Beginning

In Genesis 2:7, God began with Adam. When He created him, God did something with Adam that He did not do with Eve; He "breathed in Adam the breath of life." In this verse of scripture the Hebrew word *naphaci* (breathed) is no small thing. In a loose translation, it is God, putting part of Himself into Adam, thus causing Adam to live.

It was God's breath; it was life itself from God.

That life was not just for Adam. In that breath, the *seed* (posterity) of all human life was *entrusted* to Adam.

Eve was neither born nor created in the same way. She was taken from Adam's living tissue, from his life.

Why is this important?

Because when Adam sinned, the life of all humanity was bound within him. Therefore, when Adam ate the forbidden fruit, he sinned, and henceforth we sinned in him.

With that in mind, let's read:

> *For as in Adam all die, so also in Christ all shall be made alive.*
> 1 Cor 15:22 (NASB)

Like it or not, as men we have a *greater responsibility,* because, as it was with Adam, we are endowed with the responsibility for the life we carry for future generations.

This is no small thing.

A Natural Observation

As men, our bodies are designed to initiate life. *Our* seed is alive, even while it is within us.

A woman's seed (her egg) has all the potential for life. It has all the *raw materials* for life, but it has no life in itself. Her seed *must* be infected with life from the man in order to be made alive.

As men we carry the living seed, the seed whose origins are from the breath of God.

Notice now what the Lord told Moses.

> *And the LORD passed before him and proclaimed, "The LORD, the LORD God, merciful and gracious, longsuffering, and abounding in goodness and truth, keeping mercy for thousands, forgiving iniquity and transgression and sin, by no means clearing the guilty, visiting the iniquity of the fathers upon the children and the children's children to the third and the fourth generation".*
>
> Exo 34:6-7

As we mentioned earlier, God alone reserves the right to "visit the iniquity of the fathers" upon future generations.

Notice also that the scripture does not say "visiting the iniquity of the mothers upon the children." It clearly says "fathers," thus making reference to the fact that the responsibility for the life that goes from generation to generation is first and foremost with men.

That is why Adam's sin was different than Eve's.

One can argue the gender issue an entire lifetime. At the end of the day there is only one conclusion, the seed of human life, given by the breath of God, is passed to each generation through the loins of men.

The scriptural record is clear, a man's bloodline can be blessed because of his faithfulness, or it can be cursed as a result of his unfaithfulness.

When it comes to the penalty for unfaithfulness, the only caveat, the only saving grace, is the antiseptic power of Jesus Christ. Only He can wash away the mess, blotting out the ledger entry, to make our lives clean, and give each generation its own new beginning.

We are going to talk more about that in a moment, for now let's look at James:

> *Does a spring send forth fresh water and bitter from the same opening? Can a fig tree, my brethren, bear olives, or a grapevine bear figs? Thus no spring yields both salt water and fresh."*
>
> James 3-11

In this illustration James cautions us to keep the "fountain" pure. We understand James is talking about the things we say. Yet, just as our mouths can be illustrated as a spring-for-life, so are our bodies.

This is not a new concept. The scripture tells us that the first Adam condemned his entire lineage, but the last Adam, Jesus, came to redeem and establish *His.*

So, the question now becomes, "Whose example are we following?" Are we tainting future generations like Adam? Or, in the example of Christ, are we paving a way for our descendants to have a better life?

As men we have a greater responsibility to bring our world to the salvation of the last Adam, Jesus.

> *Nevertheless death reigned from Adam to Moses, even over them that had not sinned after the similitude of Adam's transgression, who is the figure of him that was to come.*
>
> *But not as the offence, so also is the free gift. For if through the offence of one many be dead, much more the grace of God, and the gift by grace, which is by one man, Jesus Christ, hath abounded unto many.*
>
> Rom 5:14-15 (KJV)

Note again that the scripture does not say that death reigned from Eve to Moses, but from Adam.

Notice also that the scripture does not charge Adam and Eve equally, as a *couple.* If that were so, Jesus would have needed to come with a wife, so that together they could give the gift of grace to many.

Just as sin entered the world through *one man* (singular), we all have access to the gift of grace through one Man, *Jesus.*

When we get this, when we come to accept that it was not the woman's fault, when we understand that it is *our* responsibility, when we own it, then we can become a catalyst for new life, a life rich in God's promises for future generations.

But if we behave the way Adam did, if we fail to take responsibility; well, let's look more closely at Adam's mindset.

> *And the man said, "The woman whom thou gavest to be with me, she gave me of the tree, and I did eat."*
>
> Gen 3:12 (KJV)

When he was put on the spot Adam dodged his responsibility. "That woman You gave me. . ."

Adam sinned himself, but to make matters worse, when God confronted him about it, the only right response would have been, "Yes Lord, I did." Had Adam maintained his own integrity, he could have sought the Lord's grace for himself, for his wife, and for the rest of us.

We have the power to be like either Adam, that is, the first Adam or the Last Adam—Jesus.

We learn through Adam and other biblical examples, such as Ahab (who we discuss in greater detail in a subsequent chapter), that when a man refuses to take responsibility, he brings some measure of death, not only for himself, but for generations to come.

Are women exempt from this responsibility? Certainly not. Neither is one gender better or worse than the other. The garden's fracture laid responsibility on each according to his and her God-given purpose.

> *To the woman He said: "I will greatly multiply your sorrow and your conception; in pain you shall bring forth children; your desire shall be for your husband, and he shall rule over you."*

Gen 3:16

For Eve, the seed of life, being tainted in Adam, forever reminds her of its defect. It is the place where his posterity unites with her seed; and it now bears fruit in pain.

For her the order was made clear. For the woman was made, not *less than* him, but *responsible to* the one from whom her life came—the man.

In the biblical record and in life, a man's failure to accept responsibility diminishes life both for him and those around him.

But there is good news.

When a man takes responsibility for his world, life comes back. In addition to life, there comes the restoration of not only his kingdom-potential, but the restoration of potential for *future generations.*

Becoming "a man after God's own heart" is not about our rights, it is not about our outward or physical strength, it is not about our pride. It is about our willingness to accept *responsibility.*

Responsibility and acceptance of our responsibility are part and parcel of what makes a man in God's eyes.

Do I identify with God, with His purpose, and with His heart? When He considers me, does He see true manliness or something else?

When God considers me, even more, when He considers *my children,* does He see us as a product of the first Adam or the Last?

Reflection and Discussion

1. Have you ever considered how the way you live affects your children or the people that come after you?

2. Have you ever wished you had done things different, so that the ones you love would be better off?

3. Have your ever told them that, and asked God together with them for forgiveness for the things you have done wrong?

Group leader, as the Lord leads, pray with the men in your group. Ask the Lord to repair the breach.

"Let the families and generations of these men grow in faith for the grace and confidence of Christ's redeeming blood.

That that not only the sins of these men be forgiven, but that their posteriety are given a new beginning, as members of the bloodline and family of Christ."

Amen

In today's pervasive climate of self-absorption, an alarming number of parents (especially fathers) have ceased allowing children's needs to trump their own.

Yet as parents capable of viewing life through the eyes of children recognize, responsibility is still the preeminent feature of fatherhood.

Pastor Robert Colwell
Calvary Chapel Crenshaw
Los Angeles, CA

My Faith

Now the LORD had said to Abram: "Get out of your country, from your family and from your father's house, to a land that I will show you."

Genesis 12:1 (NKJV)

It is relatively easy to have faith when everything is going just the way you imagined. It is easy to tell *somebody else* that they need faith when they are going through something.

But what about when you are the one in the fire? What about when your own life gets so rough that it makes you question how the things God promised could ever come?

On the day I got the bad-news from my doctor, Cozzette and I felt our lives were on track, though we were still waiting on a promise to have our children.

It had been fifteen years. We knew God heard our prayers, we were going in the direction He called us to, and we had His promise.

All of a sudden life turned a corner. All of a sudden every plan changed.

It was as though our promise could no longer be seen. It seemed as though for some reason God changed His mind.

I found myself taking a hard look at my faith, taking inventory to make sure there was nothing missing.

I thought about the father of faith, Abraham. What was it that made *him* different? What was it that caused God to take notice, to give him promises, and to make sure those promises came alive?

Reconciling Faith

Today we have Abraham for an example. Yet, in the day, place, and time where he grew up, the people in Abraham's world did not know God. Trusting in God must have made him feel as though he were swimming upstream.

It was a culture gone lost. They had forsaken the one true God, exchanging Him for statues they made with their hands.

There had to have been people who thought Abraham was crazy for his beliefs. His faith *must* have affected friendships as well as family.

It is hard enough to go against the current when you face the world at large. What about when you are living in a home where your faith sets you at odds with your own family? What if, to them, the very *thought* of God goes against everything they believed in, hoped in, and worked for?

That was Abraham's world.

> *And Joshua said to all the people, "Thus says the LORD God of Israel: 'Your fathers, including Terah, the father of Abraham and the father of Nahor, dwelt on the other side of the River in old times; and they served other gods.'"*
>
> Joshua 24:2 (NKJV)

We know that Abraham's father was an idolater, but what else do we know?

Genesis 11 gives us a few *basic* facts about Abraham. We know that he is Terah's son, that he lost his brother Haran. We know that after Haran died Abraham married Sarai.

We know that for some reason Abraham's father Terah set out from Ur with the family (See Acts 7) to relocate to Canaan, but stopped in Haran, where they stayed until Terah died.

Biblically that is pretty much what we know about Abraham. Up to that point there is just this seemingly insignificant mention of Abraham, in the few verses of Terah's genealogy, at the end of Genesis 11.

Then we come to chapter 12, where the Bible is no longer talking about how we got *to* Abraham, but about Abraham himself. It begins with God speaking, "Now the Lord had said to Abram . . ."

In my younger days, I would read things like that in the Bible and be amazed that there were men that actually got to speak to and hear from God. I thought these men were a special breed, that every once in a while God made somebody with the unique ability to hear Him.

Today I know that hearing from God is not reserved for a select few. Hearing from God is something He wants *all of us* to do. The way we do that is the same way we hear anyone else. We have to be in the right place when He is talking.

In Genesis 12, right off the bat we find God speaking to Abraham. That tells us something. That tells us that from the very onset of our recorded history of Abraham, he *already had* a relationship with God.

The very first thing we learn is that God talked with him. We later learn from Stephen (Acts 7) that this was *not the first time* God talked to Abraham.

Gaining Perspective

In the Jewish tradition it is said that, "You cannot have *Torah* without *Talmud.*" Though not part of the Bible, the Talmud are rabbinical commentaries which provide context for the Old Testament. Some of these commentaries give us insight into the Father of Faith.

One of the Talmud's early writers, Rabbi Hiyya, tells us that there is more to Abraham's background, and more to his story. Idol worship was not just Terah's religion—idol-making was the family business.

The Talmud goes on to tell us how Abraham suffered, and how his life was on the line *because* of his faith.

He was raised in a culture and economy steeped in idolatry. Going against his family's tradition must have caused him to think about his own future, about his security, even about his life.

When he managed the business for his father, Abraham ran off customers, and he mocked and destroyed the idols his father made.

He could have taken the low road; he could have chosen not to make waves.

Abraham could have weighed his inheritance and his father's respect against his faith. He could have decided not to take a stand for his God. But he was not looking for the easy way, he chose *the better way*.

This is the Abraham we are introduced to in Genesis 12. Out the gate, he had already established himself as a man of uncompromising faith, a man who talked with God, and a man who did what God said.

Local Motion
Faith was not just some emotion for Abraham, it caused him to *do* something.

The New Testament Hebrews' author draws examples from men who had faith. In example after example we are shown how *faith* became the motive behind the motion.

It was by faith that Abraham obeyed when God called him to leave home and go to another land that God would give him as his inheritance. He went without knowing where he was going.

Hebrews 11:8

Going Without Knowing

Like most couples, Abraham and Sarah wanted to start their family. They dreamed of having children. I am sure they spent many a day planning what their future and their family would look like.

They were still in that hope when God called them to go somewhere.

He knew their dreams. God also knew the humiliation they suffered *because* of their faith.

Imagine the critics. Imagine people mocking this couple. Imagine heartless people sarcastically asking them why they still believed, being as their faith had not produced children.

In the midst of that, almost suddenly, God showed up. And when He did, what He had to say to Abraham was essentially, "If you'll go where I tell you to go, I've got great promises in store for you."

Go. . . "And I will make you a great nation."

Go. . . "And I will bless you."

Go. . . "And I will make your name great."

Go. . . "And you *shall be* a blessing."

Go. . . "And I will bless those who bless you."

Go. . . "And I will curse them who curse you."

Go. . . "And *in you* all the families of the Earth shall be blessed."

In a world where Abraham's faith caused him to be disregarded and disrespected, each one of these promises spoke to the challenges he faced. They spoke to his present barrenness, they spoke to the mockers, and they spoke to his future posterity.

In the midst of the *problem,* God spoke to Abraham and gave him *promise.*

Fathering Faith

Abraham's faith moved him. It caused him to go. He ventured out, with nothing more than his promise from God.

He did not have all the details; he did not know *how* it was going to all work out. All he knew was that he had these promises, and wrapped somewhere within God's promise was Abraham's hope of becoming a father.

He was 75 and Sarah was 65. And even though Sarah was well past the age of child-bearing, they pressed on *because* they knew they had God's promise.

Would you be willing to do that?

What if it looked like your best days were behind you, like your hope was done? Would you still go where God wanted you to go? Would you still do what God asked you to do?

I Made It This Far

This is where it gets interesting. Abraham made it to his promised land. He built an altar to God and began to worship there.

The next thing we are told is that a famine forced Abraham to leave the land of promise, and go to Egypt.

Has that ever happened to you? Have you ever been well on your faith-walk, you have been doing what you are supposed to be doing, you are in the very place where you are supposed to be, and then all of a sudden something happens that forces you to go in *what appears to be* a different direction?

How we view what happened next is very important to our faith.

As Abraham neared Egypt he knew that the Egyptians were likely to kill him for his wife. He knew that the Pharaoh took the fairest women of the land for himself. Abraham agreed with Sarah to tell people *only* that she is his sister. Sure enough, Pharaoh got word of her beauty and took Sarah for himself.

It looks as if to save his own skin, Abraham threw Sarah under the bus. It looks like Abraham did *not* have faith, and that he failed to protect his wife.

If that were true, it would be very similar to something Adam did. But, is that what *really* happened?

The Garden Problem

In a later chapter I share how in an informal survey, most women I asked see Adam's failure to protect the Garden as the sin that condemned humanity. Let's look at how (and if) that applies here.

If the "Garden problem" were a matter of Adam failing to protect Eve, then the Father of Faith should be twice as guilty. *Adam* did not come up with the idea, he ate after his wife ate. What Abraham did was his idea, and he did it twice.

We will dive into that in better detail later. For now it is enough to say that there is a fundamental difference between Adam and Abraham. Adam put his faith in the gift (Eve), while Abraham's faith was in the Gift-giver (God).

Come Closer

When God speaks to us, when He sends us on a mission and gives us His promise, He does not always give us the *whole* picture.

Time and time again we find God restating His promise to Abraham. Each time He does that, He gives Abraham a little more insight.

At the time when famine drove Abraham to Egypt, all he knew was that God promised him descendants (Genesis 12:7). He did not know yet that having children *with* Sarah was part of that promise.

Abraham was 75 when God called him out of Haran and told him again (cp. Acts 7:1) to go to Canaan. He was full of faith and set in his ways.

This is a man who knew how to talk with God, he built altars to God, he worshipped, and he listened.

This is the man who kept to his faith, even when his life was on the line. This is the man who obeyed God all the way to his promise. Is it likely that such a man *suddenly* lost his faith just because he was going to Egypt?

Is it not more likely that when Abraham told the Egyptians that Sara was his sister, he was not trying to save himself as much as he thought he was protecting the promise of God in him? Is it not more likely that he was trying to protect his posterity?

There are times when what we hear from God is just a tiny piece of the big picture. We know what He told us is important. God is birthing something amazing and it *has to* come from us. We know it is in there, but we have not gotten close enough to understand everything yet.

While we are walking-out the promise, sometimes we do things that seem like they make sense. But, it is not until God gives us more information that we realize there is more to *the way* He wants us to get there.

Eleven years after God's original promise we find Abraham at that place again. Sarah knew she was past the age, and she gave her servant Hagar to Abraham so that God's promise could be fulfilled.

We cannot just look at this and assume that Abraham was unfaithful. Abraham acted in faith according to the way he understood his promise at that point in time.

God does not always tell us everything. Imagine if He did. If Abraham knew the famine was coming, he would have made other plans. If he knew his promise was going to come through Sarah, this man of God would have waited.

What if fathering Ishmael and this "she is my sister act" were all part of God's plan?

During the famine, Abraham could not sustain his family. Necessity caused him to go someplace he otherwise would not have gone. Because of the "sister act," Abraham and Lot returned home from Egypt so wealthy that they had outgrown their own land, and Lot had to move.

Because of the, "sister act" Abraham became an example of hope for Israel, who would also later be driven to Egypt by a famine, and would likewise come out of Egypt with her spoils.

A second time we find that Abraham traveled, telling people Sarah was his sister; and this time King Abimelech took Sarah.

This time Abraham had more information. He knew that the promise was *specifically* connected to Sarah. Does that imply this "sister act" meant he acted without faith this time?

A Faithful Background

Back in Genesis 14 we find that Abraham took 318 of his servants to battle against the armies of four kings to recover his family and their household. The Bible is clear that these kings were fierce; they had just beaten the armies of 5 other kings.

With little over 300 men, Abraham waged war against the armies of these fierce kings, and recovered his family, their people, and their belongings.

Abraham was not a fearful man, except that he had a *healthy reverence for God.*

If anything, when Abraham passed through Gerar (Genesis 20) he was confident that God would deliver both him and Sarah from King Abimelech, even as He did once before with Pharaoh. Remember, in *this* account we are told that Abraham was a prophet.

My brother please be careful here not to conclude that it is okay to forsake your wife for ministry; let's be clear—it is not.

What you should come away with today is an understanding that while Abraham was willing to continue on without Sarah, he let God clarify the promise so there was no doubt it included his wife.

Abraham was not some macho man who thought women had no say. The picture we get of Abraham is that he was a man who listened to God first and foremost.

It is not about whether Abraham thought a man should or should not listen to his wife. It is about Abraham being able to take his direction from God. It is about a man who was confident in his faith enough to accept when that direction came *through* his wife.

Perhaps one of the toughest things he ever had to do was send Ishmael away. Ishmael was his firstborn son. But, because of "baby mama drama," Sarah wanted Ishmael and *his* mother to leave.

What would you do? What if you had a previous child, and your wife told you that child could no longer live in the home with you?

Abraham did what *God said,* he held to his faith and to God's promise (Genesis 21:12).

Keeping Up the Faith

Like David, Abraham was another man just like any of us. He stood out from the crowd because he *refused to follow* the crowd. He is not a man who allowed his faith to be affected by public opinion.

There were times when he had incredible challenges, times when he just had to keep going in spite of how impossible the situation seemed.

What sets his faith apart is that *regardless* of Abraham's challenges, inadequacies, or circumstance, he listened to God, and he did what God asked of him.

Speak to Me

It is easy to be shy around someone you are not familiar with. If you are not building a faith-walk now, then when troubling times come you will feel lost, inadequate, and unable to talk to God.

Having faith does not exempt us from life's challenges. What it does is keep our promises alive *when* those challenges hit us.

Having faith does not mean you know everything. It means that you are not afraid to bring your questions and concerns to God.

But Abram said, "Lord GOD, what will You give me, seeing I go childless, and the heir of my house is Eliezer of Damascus?"

Then Abram said, "Look, You have given me no offspring; indeed one born in my house is my heir!"

Genesis 15:2-3 (NKJV)

Abraham brought his cares, he brought his concerns, he brought his passion to God; and that is what God wants *us* to do.

. . .casting all your care upon Him, for He cares for you.

1 Peter 5:7 (NKJV)

Reflection and Discussion

1.   Do you consider yourself a believer in Christ and "man of faith?"

2.   On a scale of 1 – 10, how would you rate your faith?

3.   Has God ever asked you to do something that looked as if it would cost you dearly?

4.   If God were to ask you to go somewhere you've never been, even change careers, would you go?

5.   What promises has God made you that you are still looking for?

He will herald God's arrival in the style and strength of Elijah, soften the hearts of parents to children, and kindle devout understanding among hardened skeptics—he'll get the people ready for God.

Luke 1:17 (MSG)

Identity and destiny, just like being and doing, are vitally linked. Who we are affects what we do, and vice versa.

Unfortunately for most of us men, we let corrupt desires, broken promises, and defeatist experiences define us so that our identity flows out of a sense of failure along the road of life.

It is hard to shake off a failed identity, rooted deeply in our old, sinful nature, especially when we continue to act on what we have accepted about our failed self. But Jesus changes all of that.

Identity in Christ restores the intention of God in our souls. That is why it is crucial that we reckon who we are in Him.

When we know who we are in the Lord, it makes all the difference in what we do from here, no matter from where we have come!

Galatians 2:20 (NKJV) -- I have been crucified with Christ; it is no longer I who live, but Christ lives in me; and the life which I now live in the flesh I live by faith in the Son of God, who loved me and gave Himself for me.

Dr. Jan L. Spencer, Ph.D
Former Pastor, Lancaster Foursquare Church
Superintendent, So-Cal District Foursquare Churches
Faculty Director/Associate Professor,
American Public University System
Adjunct Faculty, The King's University and
Life Pacific College

My Identity

Inner-City USA, there's a boy struggling to become a man. His father left when he was so young, the boy has no memory of him. Mother had to manage two jobs just to keep a home and put food on the table. Hard as she tried, she could never teach her son what it means to be a man.

Just outside their front door is where his world begins. The neighborhood they live in is impoverished, brutal, and unforgiving. In it there are two kinds of men, those who land a good job and move out, and those who will never leave, because of some handicap, be it emotional, physical, or financial.

For many, that life is all there is. Success or failure for them is a matter whether they make it through another day.

In one such neighborhood, many years ago, a man named Tony told me how he once walked into a police department and pulled a gun on the Desk Sargent. I asked him why he would do something like that. He said, "Because I knew if I got locked up, I would have a roof over my head and three meals a day."

Tony was regarded by some as a hero in that neighborhood. Many of the kids looked up to him.

Tony is dead now, and so are all of his brothers, and many of his friends.

Kids growing up in tough neighborhoods are no different from kids growing up anywhere else. They are trying to find themselves, they want to discover who they are. In the absence of a father figure, they will identify with whoever takes the time to show them how to survive.

Given the right guidance, at the right time, many of these kids *can* be reached.

Our ministry does a lot of work with children like these. Most of them are hoping for a brighter future.

Sadly, I've run into a few who have long since given up hope for a better life. They've become too familiar with the drug dealers, thugs, and gangs. Street life is all they understand, and has become *all they want* to know.

Suburbia USA, there's a man who struggled all his life to become successful. His car, his home, and his way of life all speak of his achievements. He's not like one of those stuck in the ghetto, he's a man of great accomplishment.

His priorities are his wife, kids, and the lifestyle they have become accustomed to. When he looks in the mirror, he sees the doctor, lawyer, or some other professional, and he says to himself, "That's who I am." Inside, he's just as lost as the boy in the ghetto.

The Man in the Mirror

We often identify with what we want to do, or what we have accomplished.

Yet, more important than what we do, more important than anything we can accomplish, is *who we are in Christ.*

In the Book of Mark, Jesus asked the question,

> *For what will it profit a man if he gains the whole world, and loses his own soul?*
>
> Mark 8:36

He then went on to say that if we are ashamed to be identified with Him here and now, then He will be ashamed of us in glory.

So, the question becomes, "What or whom do we identify with?"

From His point of view, God sees us as more than what we do for a living, and more than where we live.

Remember, some people called Jesus a Nazarene. Sure, He was from Nazareth at some point, but that's not all he was.

Others called Him "the carpenter's son." All the while, Jesus knew he was destined to be more than a Nazarene and more than a carpenter's son. Referring to Himself as "The Son of David," He clearly identified Himself as the Savior, the one who the prophets said would come from *David's house.*

So, what *should* we see when we look in the mirror?

Finding the answer to that is going to take spending some face time with God.

The Burning Bush

I'm sure if you asked Moses who he was in his early days, you would have never heard him say, "Deliverer." He grew up in the palace and was groomed for success. Yet, with all he had, he still did not know *who he was.*

It was not until he spent some face time with God that Moses discovered his true identity.

Notice, Moses didn't come down from Mount Sinai looking the same way he did when he went up. The Bible says that the glory of God changed his appearance (Reference Exodus 34).

Spending time with God will change the way people see you, and it will change the way you see *yourself.*

Even when he looked at his own reflection, Moses no longer saw the timid man with career potential who grew up in the palace. As a result of spending time with God, he could see the glory of God *in* him, *around* him, and coming *from* him.

Moses never lost his individuality. He was still the same man he always was. Only now that he spent face time with God, God's glory made his future brighter.

Notice, while he was speaking with God, Moses asked the question, "Who shall I say sent me?" Perhaps that question was Moses, in some small way, trying to size-up the Lord. Perhaps it was Moses trying to understand just how big, just how awesome our God really is.

Whatever the reason for Moses asking the question, the Lord did not answer with His title or vocation. He could have said, "I am the life-giver," which would have been a true statement. He could have also called Himself a farmer, a doctor, or He could have called Himself by any number of professions; these would have all been true.

Think about it. . . If *we* identify with each other by what we do, how could we possibly fit all that the Creator of the universe is into a single title?

"I AM THAT I AM," declared the Lord. (Ref. Exodus 3:14)

Later we are told to call Him YAH, meaning He is Lord (Psalms 68:4). Over time we are given many names to describe God. The point is that identity is *so important* that God cannot be restricted by a single title.

A Reflection of My Purpose

Keep in mind that vocation is not the same as purpose. Vocation is what we do temporarily, but our God-given purpose is the bigger picture. It is what God created us to do overall.

Our true identity and His purpose are connected, so much that some people had their names changed by God in order to better fit God's Plan.

Allowing God to say *who* you are may cost you something in the short-term, but the return is greater than you can ever imagine.

When Saul got some face time with God, God told him he had been going by the wrong name. He was not born to be Saul, he was born to be Paul.

I wonder if Saul was happy with that. He went from being Saul, meaning "desired," to Paul, meaning "small." With that name change the guy who was once a man of prominence in the temple and in his community became an insignificant outcast.

Why is that? What was it about this simple name change that changed his life? Did Paul really know what it was going to cost him?

Considering that before his name change he helped persecute those who *identified* with Jesus, I think it is safe to say that Paul knew *exactly* what he was getting into. Paul knew that more than his social status was at stake. Accepting his new identity in Christ meant putting his very life on the line. Nevertheless, he did it. He took his stand with

Him.

Sometimes we have to do that. Sometimes, when God shows us our purpose He is also telling us that it is time to take a stand.

Sure, it would have been easier not to rock the boat. Sure, he could have kept hanging out in the temple by day, and he could have gone to church at night.

But, once Paul *accepted* who he was, his former life became incompatible with the man God called him to be.

Think about it... Saul's very name went from meaning, "Mr. Big Stuff," to, "Mr. Insignificant," figuratively speaking.

Yet, after his name change, Paul went on to do his most significant work.

Empowered by his new identity, Paul went on to become a world-changer.

With Paul's name change, his life and profession completely changed course.

Most of us will not have to go to such extremes today. Most of us will never have to change professions to become who Christ called us to be. At the same time, it will always cost us *something.*

Whatever that cost is, it is a small price to pay for what we stand to gain.

And, yes, there are some who *are* in the wrong profession. My brother, if you are not in the vocation that God wants you in, you are just never going to find satisfaction, no matter how much your current job pays.

Whatever success Saul once enjoyed, as Paul he went on to become more successful than he ever could have been, had he not accepted his new identity.

Paul's name change was deliberate. Small things are important to God. God often uses the smallest things to achieve His greatest purpose.

No matter how small any of us think we are, no matter how meaningless we feel our lives are, no matter what our social standing, and no matter how insignificant the world considers us to be; when we understand who we are in Christ, we too have the potential to become world-changers!

Paul did not gripe over his name being changed. He did not cower from his new identity. Once he had his encounter with the Lord, he did not shrink into the background, he did not let that new name put him in a box, and he no longer let the world define him.

Can you see God's glory?

Our world recognizes when Christianity is a catchphrase, and not *truly* who we are. They can tell whether the cross is just some piece of jewelry we wear around our neck, or if we truly bear it on our shoulders.

Once you tell them that you're a Christian, some people will test you to see if you really are who you say you are.

Am I unafraid to walk the walk? Do I keep my Christianity a secret? Does my Christian identity only come out when it is convenient; when nobody is looking?

How does our world see us?

Spiritual Personality Dis-Order

Let's be honest. Some of us know people who had their encounter with Jesus, and they got all fixed-up on the *outside*. They talk *Christianese*, go to church on Sunday, and may have even become someone of prominence in the congregation. Yet, *inside,* they have never had an identity change.

My brother, living a double life is just not profitable. What profits more than anything, is when we completely accept the person God has destined us to be.

Behind the Scenes

Sometimes a double life is not easy to see. Sometimes in public you look like you have it all together; but your private life tells a different story. The prophet Eli is one such man.

Eli was certain to go down in history, not only because he was a prominent priest, but because of his ministry.

There was a woman named Hannah who was barren, yet God used Eli's voice to change that situation. He prophesied over her and she conceived, giving birth to Samuel the prophet.

Yet, though Eli's professional life seemed on track, his personal life told a different story. How do we know that? Let's look at First Samuel:

> *Now the sons of Eli were corrupt; they did not know the LORD.*
>   1 Sam 2:12

Perhaps Eli was tired of fussing with his boys. Perhaps he just did not know what to do with them. Perhaps he was more concerned with his status than his posterity. Whatever the reason, it would seem that to some degree, Eli was just not there for them.

Eventually, his personal failure overshadowed his accomplishments. No matter how many people his ministry helped, Eli failed to establish a proper apprenticeship at home. He failed to teach his sons the importance of who *God* called them to be. As we will see in a moment, that failure had tremendous consequences for Eli, his family, and the people.

Dual Identities

Perhaps Eli did not have much to do with raising his children, perhaps he relegated *that* job to his wife.

Why do I say that? Well, look at what happened. Look at the way Eli's children related to their world. They caused the people to despise the offering of the Lord (1 Sam 2:17).

As priests, they were supposed to be examples that others could follow. Part of that meant they were supposed to cultivate an atmosphere of worship.

Where was Eli when his sons were "trippin?"

Yes, Eli talked to his sons about what they were doing.

> *So he said to them, "Why do you do such things? For I hear of your evil dealings from all the people."*
>
> 1 Samuel 2:23

Why did Eli have to hear about what his sons were doing from the people? What was he doing, while his children were going astray?

Instead of learning right and wrong from their father, Hophni and Phinehas learned from a troubled culture. By the time Eli talked to them, it was too late—They didn't want to hear it.

Tough Love

What recourse did Eli have? Well, he could have brought them before the counsel. He could have sat Hophni and Phinehas down from their job.

But the sad commentary is Eli never took responsibility for teaching his sons to honor and obey God. Perhaps that was because he did not have a healthy relationship with God himself. The bible says he honored his children, more than God (1 Samuel 2:29).

Look what happened as a result. His failure caused a breach in Eli's posterity. And, even though he did not commit the act himself, his failure brought severe judgment to his *entire house.*

> *In that day I will perform against Eli all that I have spoken concerning his house, from beginning to end.*

For I have told him that I will judge his house forever for the iniquity which he knows, because his sons made themselves vile, and he did not restrain them.

And therefore I have sworn to the house of Eli that the iniquity of Eli's house shall not be atoned for by sacrifice or offering forever.

1 Sam 3:12-14

This is serious business!

From what we do know about Eli, I think it is safe to say that to some degree he was an absentee father.

It is easy to get caught up in the job description. It is easy to identify with everyday life so much so, that we become distracted from our true purpose.

But, identifying yourself as a person who points people *to* God brings out your best life, while being known as someone who drives people away from God causes your life to deteriorate.

Eli's sons Hophni and Phinehas learned that lesson. I'm sure they thought they were living large for a while. But, what good is it if you gain the whole world and lose your soul?

But each one is tempted when he is drawn away by his own desires and enticed. Then, when desire has conceived, it gives birth to sin; and sin, when it is full-grown, brings forth death.

James 1:14-15

My brother, if you do not know already who God called *you* to be, spend some face time with Him.

Once He tells you who you are, own it completely. If you are willing to do that, if you are willing to be true to who God says you are, you are destined to become a world-changer.

Reflection and Discussion

1. Who are you?

2. Who were your childhood influences and what impressed you about them?

3. Who are your mentors today?

4. Have you ever avoided doing what's right, because you didn't want to give the wrong impression?

5. After you are gone, how will people remember you?

*P*erception is reality to the perceiver. With that said, every man has his own definition of masculinity. However, every man has a level of privacy that will protect and maintain his level of manhood, no matter what he has to do to cover for it, and this changes as we get older and we begin to understand the true reality of life.

I am now over 80 years old and I realize that the more open I am, the more my masculinity is protected. It is protected by truth, and truth is protected by God. After all, whether I am strong or weak, I am His son.

How I look to the world determines my drawing power to the kingdom of God (Matt 5:16).

So, I urge every man to be true to himself, but to ask God to help him become the image of His son Jesus Christ as said in Romans 8:29;

> 'For whom he did foreknow, he also did predestinate to be conformed to the image of his Son, that he might be the firstborn among many brethren.'

You can't miss being a man among men in the image of His Son.

Bishop Henry W. Hearns
Former Senior Pastor
Living Stone Cathedral of Worship
Littlerock, CA
Mayor Emeritus Lancaster, CA

www.HenryHearns.org

My Defense

There was a man in the land of Uz, whose name was Job; and that man was blameless and upright, and one who feared God and shunned evil.

(Job 1:1)

While getting ready to go into surgery one day I was laying on a gurney in the pre-op area.

My doctor was seated on a chair just to my right. His arms were spread atop the bed rail with his hands clasped together. His chin was resting in his hands, and his face was no more than a few inches from mine.

Prep for that procedure included a week of fluids; so when time came for the actual surgery, my bladder was working overtime. When I could hold it no more, I glanced over at the doctor, who was already invading my space, and told him that I needed to use the restroom before we got started.

He then handed me a small plastic container and said, "Here you go." I expected him to at least turn his head, but he never did. He just sat there, perched on the bed rail, just as he had been.

It was quite a challenge, trying to stay cloaked under the flimsy hospital gown while using the bedside urinal. Watching me struggle with that, out of nowhere, the doctor began to chuckle. "What's so funny?" I asked. With that he gestured towards the operating room and said, "In a few seconds we are going to be in there, and there is nothing we will not see."

The doctor was referring to my vain attempt to cover up, in the face of a procedure that was going to more than strip me of all modesty.

Looking back, I see the humor. I mean, there I was laying on a gurney, getting ready to be operated on, and all I could think about was defending my privates.

Modesty did not matter at that point, nor did the events that led up to that moment. All that mattered, was that right there, the only thing I needed to do was surrender. I needed to resolve myself to the fact that it was not the time to worry about being exposed.

I suppose there was still a choice. I could have stuck to my guns, so to speak. I could have decided right there that I was not going to allow myself to become any more vulnerable than I had already become.

I could have defended myself altogether; I could have called off the surgery.

I had to make a decision. Do I take back control? Do I defend myself while I still can? Or, do I surrender completely, trusting even my very life to the care of the doctor?

Often times we are faced with decisions like that. We feel that if we stay on our present course somebody may see something we do not want them to see. When that happens, do we hang in there and risk further exposure? Do we allow ourselves to become even more vulnerable? Do we defend ourselves at all?

Could it be that at *precisely* those moments God has *something else* in mind?

It is often during those vulnerable moments that God is about to do something. It is like He is going through the pre-op checklist. He is getting us all ready, then just when He is ready to operate, up come the covers.

It is not always obvious. It may not even be a conscious attempt to hide something. It may be just as simple as an automatic reaction, defending some part of our life that suddenly becomes exposed.

Most of us have some defensive reflex. We can become defensive the moment that certain button is pushed.

The problem is that when the covers come up we get in the way of our own remedy.

With that in mind, let's look at Job. Here is a man who by all accounts revered God and lived upright.

In Job 6:8 we find God Himself telling us that Job had greater moral character than any man on earth. That is not to say Job was perfect. It merely points out Job was *more righteous* than anyone else.

Perhaps in that pre-operative condition God saw in Job something that could *only* be made better with his life laid open. Perhaps the whole book of Job is merely God's operating procedure; a prescription for the cutting away of some defect, in order to bring about healing of the things that were keeping him from becoming the best God envisioned he could be.

It was not Job's sin that caused the tragedies that plagued him. God knew that Job could endure the process and come out better.

Remember, God Himself offered Job up for Satan's consideration. That was not God setting Job up for a demotion. As it turns out, He was actually preparing Job for promotion!

To Job, I am sure it did not seem like a promotion was coming. I am sure there were moments it must have seemed like all of his life's work had been vain. He was stripped of everything. . . His posterity, his prosperity, and by the time all was said and done, Satan had taken everything except his very life.

There he was, minding his own business, when in an instant Job lost everything he had worked for. All of the things which once testified of his uprightness and success; his family, his wealth, and his home, were all lost. Eventually even Job's health hung in the balance, and he was plagued with sores over his whole body.

The life that he once knew had become a distant memory. Not only were the tangible things gone, but by all appearance, the sun was setting on any future ambitions he may have had.

Has that ever happened to you? Have you ever been in a place where it looked like you had little to nothing left? A place where it looked like all that remained were the memories of how things *used to be?*

Job's life turned the corner. In nearly an instant he went from being a successful man, a man of many accomplishments, to this desolate, afflicted, and vulnerable shell of a man.

Perhaps the only thing that could have brought relief to Job in that suffering would have been some measure of compassion from his friends. Instead, they judged him according to his circumstance. They looked at his outward condition and argued that he *must have* brought it on himself.

Perhaps many of us can relate to what *Job's friends* were thinking.

Yet, if you look closely you see that Job did not deserve that situation any more than anyone else. In fact, one could argue he deserved it *less.* Remember, he was *more righteous* than everyone else.

What about the conversation he was having with his friends? Is that where his sin was? Were his answers to his friends wrong?

Even if Job's answers were wrong, what he said had nothing to do with his condition. Job was already afflicted when he had that conversation.

Job's answers were not *technically* wrong. Though Job may have come across as self-righteous, there is little to suggest that what he said to his friends was actually wrong. He was simply stating the facts.

Looking at this conversation between Job and his friends, it is easier, at least for me, to see that Job's friends were the ones with the more serious problem.

Job's friends had a lot of information *about* God and about Job, but they lacked compassion. They had the lingo, but they did not have the insight. Before passing judgement, they did not stop and ask God what *He* was doing.

Speaking "words without knowledge," they were more concerned with setting Job straight, than having the grace needed to comfort their hurting friend.

Let's face it; there are times when it is clear that we are reaping the harvest from bad decisions.

Honestly, have you ever thought to say, "Aha!" When somebody who did wrong finally got what they deserved?

That is what Job's friends *assumed* they were dealing with, someone who just made life bad for himself.

Yes, there are times when we reap from bad judgment. But, there are also times when we are just going through, times when we are being set-up for a divine lift-up.

It is dangerous to jump to conclusions in view of *somebody else's* hardships. It is dangerous to measure someone else's struggle solely by your own experience.

I remember just before the doctors diagnosed me with lung-disease, I had to take a lot of time off work. One day a coworker and I sat down to talk. What he had to say was essentially that since *he* felt fine, there was no reason *I* should be off work. He was judging my health according to his own condition!

My friends testimony is one thing, but it is wrong to make yourself the standard for others to live by.

So, what do you do when it all hits the fan, and someone you know is having a difficult time? How can you be *God's man* for them? What do you say to him or her?

Paul gives us some clues here in Second Corinthians:

> *Not that we are sufficient of ourselves to think of anything as being from ourselves, but our sufficiency is from God, who also made us sufficient as ministers of the new covenant, not of the letter but of the Spirit; for the letter kills, but the Spirit gives life.*
>
> 2 Cor 3:5-6

In this passage we can see that God is not interested in our ability to win the debate; He wants us to have the *right spirit*. The right spirit is neither legalistic nor condemning. The right spirit is uplifting, it brings life.

Competition

Let's face it, some of us are more competitive than others. But, if we are in a competitive mode, it is easy to see a wounded brother as easy pickings.

God wants all of us to know Him. When we are graceful to others, two things happen. First, we show the world that we *do in fact* know Him. Second, *we make Him known.*

Our world was already condemned before Jesus came, yet He said, "For God did not send His Son into the world to condemn the world, but that the world through Him might be saved" (John 3:17).

Now, if *He* did not come into the world to condemn the world, where do any of us get off thinking that is *our* job?

With that in mind, when someone is hurting, when someone is really facing life's challenges, does my response, however true and however accurate, does it minister *grace?*

When someone is hurting as a result of something they did wrong, that person usually knows what they did. My religious rants in their face are of little use to help that person.

We all go through hard times. Sometimes we bring those hard times on ourselves, and sometimes we do not.

I would venture to say that most of us have never experienced the fullness of Job's suffering. Yet, at some level, many of us have thought, "I can relate."

Yet, the story of Job has less to do with Job's problems, than it does the *process.* If we can relate to anything, it is the fact that all of us face challenges.

Job eventually found restoration. There is no simple one or two part formula here. Let's look at several factors that work together to bring about Job's (and our) restoration.

Reverence

Certainly Job was careful to reverence God. Yet, even in that he was still missing something.

> *The fear of the LORD is the beginning of knowledge, but fools despise wisdom and instruction.*
>
> Prov 1:7

Proper reverence of God and knowing what is important to Him is something that should be important to each of us.

Paul said it this way, "I delight in the Law of God according to the inner man" (Romans 7:22).

The scriptural record shows us that Job had a healthy fear of the Lord, and he was a righteous man.

His friends were not witness to, nor did they have any witness that could say that Job had sinned. For them, it was pure speculation, presumption that his plight could *only* be caused by sin against God.

Think about it. Job was more righteous than his friends. Yet, even with that Job lost just about everything. His body covered in sores, the only thing he had left was the reputation he once enjoyed, the memory of how he lived an upright life before God.

There was nothing left of his life that could be hidden, there was no family left to protect him. He had become a mere shell of a man.

Job's life had been laid open. He was more vulnerable than ever before. And, that is the place where he made his defense, his last stand. Job was trying to protect whatever semblance of modesty he had left, even if it was just a memory.

Technically, Job answered his friends with the truth. But, there was something going on deeper, something that is perhaps not as easily translated by pen and parchment. It can only be seen near the end of the conversation, when God joined in. That is the defensive posture of Job's heart crying out, "I do not deserve this."

Prior to his trial, with all of his efforts to walk upright before God, there had to be some sense that he had sown good seed and was entitled to a good harvest.

If you read carefully through Job's defense, you can almost hear him saying, "This was not supposed to happen to me."

Though we are sometimes tempted to think that way, with all that any of us thinks he is entitled to, how many of us can truthfully say that he walked his entire life as righteous as Job?

Yet, all of Job's righteousness could not bring the healing he needed.

Why?
Because God reserves the right to be Lord.

So you might ask, "Well, what good did Job's righteousness do for him?"

What it did was help him endure the process.

In the final analysis, we have no entitlement credits, only a *responsibility* to hear and follow the voice of our God at any given moment.

The Peter Pride Principle

Peter was a passionate man. He had great zeal for the Lord. But, that zeal was often expressed inappropriately. Peter had a tendency to jump the gun.

Imagine, Peter thought that he was strong enough to draw his sword to defend Jesus! There had to be a dimension of pride at work here. Imagine the vanity of thinking that *his* abilities could somehow save our Savior!

The challenge for Peter, Job, and, I believe most of us, is to be *ready and able to do,* yet willing to wait on the Lord. That way, when the battle presents itself (and it certainly will), we can allow Him to do what a Savior does. . . That is to bring *us* deliverance.

Peter misplaced his purpose. It was not Peter's job to be the Savior's savior; nor is it ours. The battle, remember, is the Lord's.

It is not our battle when the flood tides come and our enemy comes from every side. . . It is the Lord's.
It is not our battle when people talk about us. . . It is the Lord's.

It is not our battle when we are not getting along with our family. . .

It is the Lord's.

It is not our battle.   No, the battle is not ours, it is the Lord's.

Peter was busy reacting instead of hearing what Jesus was saying. As a result he injured someone else in the very place of his own defect, he cut off someone's ear.

While Job was busy defending himself, he was not hearing from God either. In this sense, neither Peter nor Job were listening to God when they took their stand.

In the questions that God asked him, Job realized that he was making a vain attempt to defend himself. He didn't need to defend himself. What he needed was a Savior.

"Where were you," God said, "when I laid the foundations of the Earth?" It is as though God was saying, "It is My fight Job, do not even try!"

Just as Job and all the rest of us ultimately learn, our deliverance only comes to whatever extent we trust *in Him.*

Perhaps there is a man reading this today who has been feeling that he is in a situation he did not bargain for, that what once seemed promising, now seems faded. You find yourself fighting and fighting, winning and losing, struggling and sinking.

In the beginning there was this great hope and trust that you were doing what God told you to do. But, now you question whether you heard from Him at all.

How many other decisions have you made knowing that God was leading you, but later, because of the "operation," you began to question whether you were hearing from God in the first place?

Right now, do you find yourself being defensive? Right where you are, does it seem like all hope is lost?

Running away does not solve the problem. Running away from a problem is just another way of covering it up, of trying to make sure people will not see your weakness.

Just as in Job's day, right now, in response to your discouragement there should come a sense of God saying, "Where were you when I created your world?"

When the morning stars sang together, and all the sons of God shouted for joy, where were you?

Have you given the horse strength? Have you clothed his neck with thunder? Where were you, when God set the limits of the seas?

Where were you my brother? Where were you, oh man of God?

In response to Job's hurt, God asked questions that made him examine the stand he was taking.

Job got it. He recognized that God, and not Job, has the ultimate entitlement over all of creation. He realized that God's strength is above all, and Job *yielded* his struggle to the awesomeness of his Creator.

Confronted by the voice of the Lord, as though face to face, Job's conversation and demeanor changed instantly, as he answered:

> *Listen, please, and let me speak; You said, 'I will question you, and you shall answer Me. I have heard of You by the hearing of the ear, but now my eye sees You. Therefore I abhor myself, and repent in dust and ashes.*
>
> Job 42:4-6

When questioned by God, Job's posture changed from self-defense to total surrender.

What happened as a result?

His restoration came.

It was not until Job stopped trying to defend himself that there came an outpouring of new life.

Is there ever a time to defend yourself? Of course, but only when you know for certain God is the one telling you to do it.

My brother, there is life in humility, and in our humility we trust God.

There is liberty in the knowledge that God knows exactly where we are at any given moment. There is freedom in not having to fight to make ourselves more relevant than we really are. And, that liberty, that freedom comes alive for the people in our world when we lower our defenses and allow Him to be our Defender, our Savior.

Could Job have been restored sooner? I believe so.

Having the Right Spirit

In His "Sermon on the Mountain" Jesus began by letting us know that there is a blessing for being "poor in spirit." In other words, being high-spirited will *keep us from* His blessings.

Matthew chapter 5 could be almost be titled, "Let Down Your Defense." The heart of the chapter is centered on issues that arise from a defensive posture rather than reliance on God.

Jesus declares,

> *Agree with your adversary quickly, while you are on the way with him, lest your adversary deliver you to the judge, the judge hand you over to the officer, and you be thrown into prison. Assuredly, I say to you, you will by no means get out of there till you have paid the last penny.*
>
> Matt 5:25-26

There is no heavenly prize here for a winning argument. For us, there is only *more* bondage whenever we choose to be defensive.

We have to be willing to lay down our arms, <u>inquire of the Lord,</u> and trust Him to lead us. The result of *that kind* of faith is freedom.

God's word is sharper than any surgeon's scalpel. But if we defend ourselves when He did not tell us to, we take the scalpel from Him. Becoming a man after God's own heart means re-training our minds to think and react, not the way that we once reacted, not the way we think a man is supposed to react, but setting our hearts to react the way Jesus wants us to.

With this in mind, let's look at Isaiah:

> *He was oppressed and He was afflicted, yet He opened not His mouth; He was led as a lamb to the slaughter, and as a sheep before its shearers is silent, so He opened not His mouth.*
>
> Isa 53:7

Jesus understood His purpose. As He was put on trial and led to the cross, He demonstrated this principle of trusting God to be His defender. He knew what was at stake. Yet, to Him, the trial He was facing was only a "momentary light affliction."

As a result of Jesus' surrender there came an outpouring of life. It was resurrection life, not only for Him, but for His entire world.

Let us so learn to trust in God, that it becomes second nature to submit all defense to Him.

Reflection and Discussion

1. Have you ever felt like you were being punished for something that you didn't deserve?

2. What are your "hot buttons," the things that make you become defensive in a hurry?

3. Has being defensive ever cost you something - A relationship, job, or an opportunity?

4. What would you do different next time?

Small Group Prayer

Seperate into small groups and pray for one another.

Pray that the Lord forgive us for the times we let our defensiveness get in His way. Pray that He takes away the "triggers," that cause us to act before consulting with or hearing from Him. Pray for the leadership of His Holy Spirit to replace our defensive tendencies.

Every man aspires to greatness in some form or fashion. Typically, such greatness is associated with "doing something" that has significance. This passion for significance is intertwined with a man and his ministry.

When I hear the word "ministry" it inspires a wide range of ideas that range from the "biggie" of a specific calling from God to simply lending a helping hand. Those two ideas and everything in between can be a ministry. The word ministry simply means to render a service. In essence, a man and his ministry is about a man making the quality decision to be a servant in all areas of life where he lives and exists. This kind of significance comes from enriching the lives of others rather than self-service and personal gratification.

It is imperative that a man discovers what the specific call for ministry that God has for his life. However, it is equally important that he live each day lending a helping hand wherever he finds himself. In fact this daily availability to lend a hand may comprise the "mother-load" of ministry opportunities.

Significance comes in both big and small packages, but who can say what looks the biggest to God? Maybe the more spectacular from God's perspective is the service rendered in the "dailies." One thing is undeniable – Jesus said, "Whoever desires to be great among you shall be your servant" Mark 10:42.

If a man desires to do something significant that catches the attention of God, then he must choose the path of a servant. When a man chooses the path of a sacrificial servant he has aligned himself with the path of the Savior.

Jesus said in Mark 10:45, "For even the Son of Man came not to be served, but to serve, and to give his life a ransom for many." Being a servant is the seedbed of significance for a man and his ministry.

It worked for Jesus, surely it will work for us as well!

Reverend Kim Pitner
Missional Director
MidSouth District of Foursquare Churches

My Ministry

Now the sons of Eli were corrupt; they did not know the LORD. And the priests' custom with the people was that when any man offered a sacrifice, the priest's servant would come with a three-pronged fleshhook in his hand while the meat was boiling. Then he would thrust it into the pan, or kettle, or caldron, or pot; and the priest would take for himself all that the fleshhook brought up. So they did in Shiloh to all the Israelites who came there.

Also, before they burned the fat, the priest's servant would come and say to the man who sacrificed, "Give meat for roasting to the priest, for he will not take boiled meat from you, but raw." And if the man said to him, "They should really burn the fat first; then you may take as much as your heart desires," he would then answer him, "No, but you must give it now; and if not, I will take *it by force." Therefore the sin of the young men was very great before the LORD, for men abhorred the offering of the LORD.*

1 Sam 2:12-17

Not everybody was born to be a pastor, not everybody has a vocational ministry. Yet, all of us have a ministry of some kind.

If you have ever thought God has called you to vocational ministry, "On the Road to Glory: Finding Your Inner Dream" is a book you will enjoy.

Whether you are a husband, father, choir member, church council member, or preacher, you have a ministry. And, your understanding of *how* your ministry and your faith work together will impact the people around you.

Building a good Philosophy of Ministry

Faith in God is our foundation. The boundaries of our faith are formed by our ability to hear what He is saying.

How then shall they call on Him in whom they have not believed? And how shall they believe in Him of whom they have not heard? And how shall they hear without a preacher?
Romans 10:14 (NKJV)

The point is, before you trust, you have to listen. But unless Christ's Word is preached, there is nothing to listen to.
Romans 10:17 (MSG)

In much the same way that our homes needs *more* than a foundation, having faith is not the end of our Christian walk.   It is just *the beginning.* Just like a foundation, our faith gives us something to build upon.

As we put our faith into practice we get to know God better. That is how we build on our *spiritual* foundation.

To help us build we have God's written word - The Bible. That is what the Bible is, a set of tools for growing, for helping us to learn right from wrong, <u>not as we count right and wrong</u>, but as *He* does.

> *All Scripture is given by inspiration of God, and is profitable for doctrine, for reproof, for correction, for instruction in righteousness.*
>
> 2 Timothy 3:16 (NKJV)

Getting It Right

We all come from different places. Because we are so diverse, we often see things differently. Each of us takes what we know and hear, and we put our own *spin* on it.

But does it fly?

To better illustrate this, let's take a look at some basic principles I picked up while working in the aircraft industry.

That amazing experience taught me that getting the job done right takes more than just knowing *how* to turn a wrench. The life of every flying passenger depends on whether each bolt was tightened to exact specifications, regardless of the strength of who it was that turned the wrench.

Simply *knowing* how the parts fit together is not enough. Just because you have the know-how, or even the right tools, it does not mean that you can do something as simple as tightening any aircraft bolt properly. The wrench itself has to be *calibrated* in such a way that no matter who turns it, the same force is applied.

Calibration is a process where you measure your tool against a known standard. A tool that is "out of calibration" can usually be adjusted in order to make it measure accurately.

Calibration has an expiration date. Every torque wrench used in aircraft has a sticker that lets both the mechanic and inspector know when it was last calibrated, and when it must be checked again.

Our spiritual life is much the same way. In order to have a *good theology*, we have to stay calibrated. For Christians, that happens when we study the Bible. Without a *regular diet* of bible study, all we have to work with is our un-calibrated perspective. In short, without regular calibration, more than likely, we're putting the wrong "spin" on God.

Let's say you have done that, let's say you have developed a good Bible study routine and your theology is sound. Does that mean you are ready to fly? Is there *anything else* you should think about?

Continuing with our aircraft analogy, even if someone manages to build an airplane properly it does not mean they are ready to go out and fly it. Why? Because it takes *one* license to build an airplane, and *another* license to fly.

Flying takes more than just knowing *about* aircraft. If you really want to fly, you need experience and training in fields like navigation and weather. You have to know how to calculate weight and balance, and you have to be proficient in numerous other disciplines which have nothing to do with the airplane itself. If you fail to do that, if you want to fly but you do not first gain *all* the experience required for piloting, your airplane is not likely to ever reach its destination.

In the same way, even if you have a strong theology it is entirely possible for your ministry to be off course. The reason for this is that you can know a lot *about* God and still not truly know what to do *with* that knowledge.

You can fully understand your favorite passages of scripture, even hear God when He speaks to you. But if you do not *apply* what He said, then you are completely off course (Ref Matt 13:13).

> *For if anyone is a hearer of the word and not a doer, he is like a man observing his natural face in a mirror; for he observes himself, goes away, and immediately forgets what kind of man he was.*
>
> *But he who looks into the perfect law of liberty and continues in it, and is not a forgetful hearer but a doer of the work, this one will be blessed in what he does.*
>
> James 1:23-25 (NKJV)

Illustration

In my first pastorate there was a woman who was very busy helping the ministry. She was well versed in scripture and was kind to others in the church.

Her husband also helped, and on occasion I needed to call him at home. Whenever the wife answered, before she knew it was her pastor on the line, she was quite mean. Once she recognized it was me, she transformed into the person I knew from church.

From this example we can see that our theology is one thing, but *how we live out* what we know is something else altogether.

Eli's Ministry

We have learned that Eli's sons were corrupt. We also know that they were priests (see 1 Sam 1:3). Aside from that, what qualifications did they have?

Perhaps they assumed that because they were raised in the church, because they often observed priests, that being a priest was an easy job, and that anybody could do it.

Perhaps they were somehow expected to inherit a good philosophy of ministry from their father.

Perhaps they met all the academic requirements, maybe they passed all the right tests.

Whatever they had to go through to be priests, however much they accomplished on-the-job, they were not meeting the most basic job requirement. *They did not know God.*

I venture to say that God did not call Eli's sons to be priests. Somewhere along the way, this had to be a man-made decision. Perhaps there was another way these two could have served, without being the ones involved with the offering.

Straighten Up and Fly Right

I know many professional pilots, and they are a different breed. When you go to their home, you see pictures of airplanes on the walls, you find model airplanes on the shelves, there are pilot's magazines scattered all around, and there is probably even an airplane or two sitting in their garage.

One thing all professional pilots I know have in common is a *passion* for flying. These are people who are dedicated. They want to learn and know as much as they can about aircraft and flying. Everything about the way they think, even their outlook on life, their entire *philosophy,* is affected by the love they have for what they do.

When I am riding on an airplane, I do not want a pilot who is any less dedicated.

That is a big part of how you know someone is doing what God has called them to, because of the passion they have for it. It is not about the money, they are doing it because it comes natural. They are doing it because God has given them a vision, and they cannot see themselves doing anything else.

Putting it in Practice

In short, your philosophy of ministry is how you *apply* your theology. It telegraphs whether you truly love God, and how well you really know (or want to know) Him. More than anything else, it tells people what your passion is *really* about.

It did not matter how much Hophni and Phinehas knew *about* God, their philosophy of ministry was flawed.

Having a good philosophy of ministry will get you and the people who are closest to you on the safest route to God's blessings.

If you are just going through the motions, if your ministry does not grow out of your dedication to Him, it is like being a suicidal pilot who really does not like flying.

You cannot fake this. No matter how popular you are at the moment, if you are not dedicated to the Lord, if you do not want *His Spirit* leading you, if you do not want to truly know Him, each time you crash and burn you take the people that care about you down with you.

In verse 12 of our text we see that "the sons of Eli were corrupt; they did not know the LORD." By verse 17 we see what happened as a result, "men abhorred the offering of the LORD."

Giving is a vital component of worship. It is part of how we function as members of God's team. Where people don't "freely give," they miss tangible opportunities to receive from God.

Wherever people despise worship, they become negative, down, oppressed, and unable to reach their full potential. God considers that serious business.

Because they caused people to despise the offering, Eli's sons created problems for themselves and for God's people.

What am I busy doing?

In the New Testament (Matthew 25) we find a man who buried his talent. In the New King James Version, Jesus referred to this man as "lazy," but what do we really know about him?

The Greek word for lazy here is *okneros*, and comes from the root word for tardy. We do not know that this man was lazy in the way we consider laziness, but we do know that he did not produce the expected results in the *time allotted.*

My Dad often said, "We have to work smarter, not harder." For all we know, this man in Matthew 25 was a busy bee, managing a slew of programs that produced something, without giving *his boss* what he wanted.

My friends, it is entirely possible to be a busy, hard-working person, even a hard-worker in your church, and still bury your talent.

It can easily be said, that Eli's sons had great potential. Yet, however busy, however involved they were in ministry, their talent was effectively buried.

Profession Vocation and Calling

The first step in having an effective ministry is to know what you are *supposed* to be doing, and do that.

As we said, all of us have a ministry. However not everybody is *called* to vocational ministry. It is important to know what it is that God wants *you to do.*

We discuss in another volume how important it is to "stay in your lane." This cannot be over emphasized.

Some people have difficulty understanding that though we are all called to *some level* of ministry, we are not all called to the same *office.*

God does things "decently and in order," and He expects us to do the same. If we are attentive to Him, we should be able to hear God. But it is wrong to assume that when God tells *us* something, that everyone else *should* hear the same thing.

In other words, if your ministry is to be a father, then God will speak to you in *that* office. It is wrong to assume that because you hear God speaking to *you* as a father, that you know everything God should be saying to your father, your pastor, or anyone else.

For Parishioners

We have examples both within scripture and without of what *not to do* in the priesthood. Yet, that does not mean we have license to buck up against our own church leadership when we *perceive* they did not do something just right.

Will your pastor ever make a mistake? Well, did David? Did Moses? What about the father of faith, Abraham?

All of us have dual-citizenship. We all answer the call to ministry while we live in the flesh. Your pastor is no different.

Yes, your pastor has a high level of accountability. But, to God alone he stands or falls. God knows how to deal with your leader, and at the same time He knows how to use your leader to get you to where you need to go.

From bondage to promise

The Exodus was about God getting His people out of bondage and bringing them to their promise. In doing that, He assigned leaders. Not everybody was happy with God's choice.

> *They came as a group and confronted Moses and Aaron, saying, "You have overstepped yourself. This entire community is holy and GOD is in their midst. So why do you act like you are running the whole show?"*
>
> Numbers 16:3 (MSG)

Israel's journey to their promise could have taken four days. Instead they were lost in the desert for forty years. It was not Moses' failures that caused them to be lost. It was the congregation's disobedience to the voice of God spoken *through* Moses that kept them lost.

Consider that your very hope today is in the grace of God. With that in mind, as much as is within you, be *graceful* to your pastor.

Remember, if you are hearing from God, then you are likely already in the church that God has called you to. If that is the case, then your pastor has been given authority by God to lead you.

The Dathan Committee

It is not that rebellious people don't want to follow their leader, they simply do not want to follow God. They point out their leader's weakness and say things like, "If I were in charge. . ."

I call these the "Dathan Committee." What it really comes down to for them is a power struggle, and that is rebellion, plain and simple.

When God appoints a leader, that leader is God's choice. As such his authority and abilities come not from his own skills, but from God.

To make a leader, God does not need a person's resume, and He certainly does not need our approval. No, that's the way the world does things, that's not the way God typically operates.

God makes ministry leaders *in spite of* personal accomplishments, failures, strengths, and weaknesses. Remember Moses stuttered and was a murderer, while David's own father thought David so unqualified, he didn't even present him as a candidate to be king.

That is not to say God will not use someone's abilities, but that He does not *need* them. All He needs is for us to have a willing heart, He wants us dedicated to Him.

Can you spot God's heart in this scripture?

> *Come not against Mine anointed ones, and against My prophets do not evil.*
>
> 1 Chronicles 16:22 (YLT)

When God anoints someone and sends them to you, be it a pastor, a youth leader or someone else, whether or not that leader is taking the group in the direction that *you think* they should go is not the issue. What is important is that God finds you faithfully doing *your job.*

The Dathan Committee always ends up the same. In the end, God exposes them and repays them for the trouble they caused their pastor. Once God steps in, their own potential, and sometimes even their lives, are radically cut short.

For Dathan, Korah, and their cohorts, the irony is that they had a worldly philosophy of ministry, and their very lives ended with the world literally eating them alive (See Numbers 16:32).

The Hebrews author says it this way:

> *Obey those who rule over you, and be submissive, for they watch out for your souls, as those who must give account. Let them do so with joy and not with grief, for that would be unprofitable for you.*
>
> Hebrews 13:17 (NKJV)

Will there ever be a time when you need to confront your pastor?

If that time ever comes and your pastor has truly done wrong, you are not in rebellion if you handle it God's way:

> *Moreover if your brother sins against you, go and tell him his fault between you and him alone. If he hears you, you have gained your brother. But if he will not hear, take with you one or two more, that by the mouth of two or three witnesses every word may be established.*
>
> Matthew 18:15-16 (NKJV)

Remember, a witness is not somebody you managed to persuade to agree with you. A witness is somebody who has first-hand knowledge of the facts.

If someone ever comes to you with complaints about their pastor, here is the biblical prescription:

> *Do not listen to a complaint against a leader that isn't backed*

up by two or three responsible witnesses.

1 Timothy 5:19 (MSG)

Your pastor will likely appreciate your willingness to handle matters according to *biblical guidelines.*

To pastors and leaders - Every person has a ministry. That means every person has a vision. Each of us is pre-programmed for a God-given purpose.

A good understanding of *our own* purpose, <u>as well as</u> the purpose God has in the people He sends to us, will help protect us from getting off-course, crashing, or burying our talents.

Our vision is not the only vision in our ministries. If we try to ignore, erase, avoid, invalidate, or re-program someone else's vision so that it fits into ours, that person will become discontent.

Consider that when somebody joins your organization, be it secular or ministry, that person joins in the hope of *their purpose* coming alive.

People need to know that they matter to you. They need to know that *their* hopes and dreams matter to you.

When someone's vision is not nurtured, if that person does nothing more than help advance *your* vision, he or she will likely begin to feel like they are dying on the vine. If that is happening, *you* have buried talents.

Back to our example

Hophni and Phinehas are extreme examples, they were the end of the line, so-to-speak, for Eli's ministry. They were Eli's sons, and they were priests. Yet, they put their own gratification above the people they were called to serve. As a result, the people became discontent in their giving and service to the Lord.

In short, if your philosophy of ministry is only about *your* vision, that is not ministry – That is masturbation.

A healthy ministry leader is not just in it to stroke his own ego. His goal is to reproduce in the likeness of God. He is concerned that the people he leads are on the right path to the purpose and calling God has for *them.* He is passionate to encourage others to reach their vision and achieve the full measure and hope of Christ in them.

Irony or Justice?

Hannah was barren and prayed that God would give her a child, but not just any child, one she could dedicate to God.

In contrast, Eli, the High priest who prayed for Hanna, had two sons who were *not* dedicated to God. As a result they were *spiritually barren*. While Hanna conceived and gave birth to a true prophet, Eli's sons were becoming enemies of God, thus condemning Eli's lineage for all eternity.

Perhaps Eli never took the time to consider the true purpose God had for Hophni and Phinehas. Nevertheless, we know that God held Eli accountable for his son's flawed philosophy of ministry.

Notice that even while Eli was failing personally, as High Priest, he was still God's anointed. God still spoke through him to answer

Hannah's prayer, and bring life to her barren womb. As a result Hannah gave birth to Samuel. Samuel grew and went on to succeed Eli, becoming the priest and judge that God used to anoint David as King.

In spite of Eli's issues, God still used him to answer Hannah's prayers, even while Eli was forfeiting *his own* promise.

No matter how you look at it, Eli was in the wrong and people knew it. It is safe to say in that climate it would have been easy for Hanna to reject Eli as High Priest. She could have said, "let someone else pray for me – Someone who is better qualified." Had she done that, two books in the Bible would tell someone else's story, instead of her son Samuel's.

Empty Wombs

Finally, let's look for a moment at how barrenness affected *another* couple in scripture:

> *Now when Rachel saw that she bore Jacob no children, Rachel envied her sister, and said to Jacob, "Give me children, or else I die!"*
>
> Genesis 30:1 (NKJV)

Unless you are someone who has been through it, unless you have felt the pain in your wife's tears, you likely do not appreciate the agony of barrenness.

We all have a *vision* we need to give birth to.

Many people will only see Christ *in us* to the extent we demonstrate that we are willing to help *them* discover and achieve their vision – even if it means setting aside what we perceive as our own.

Yes, our people need to be on board with our vision. At the same time, it is not about *our* kingdom, it is about *His.*

Jesus said,

> *And I, if I am lifted up from the earth, will draw all peoples to Myself.*
>
> John 12:32 (NKJV)

Jesus did not have to go there. He did not have to be lifted up. Because of what He did for us at Calvary, He became the example for all of *our* ministries.

If we are helping others reach *their* God-given purpose, they will be drawn to Him and they will find *our* ministry rewarding.

In the end, some people will have ministries of their own to launch. That is not a bad thing, and it is nothing to be afraid of.

What an incredible legacy, to be able to say that your ministry helped birth healthy ministries!

Jesus could have done things differently. He could have stayed (in the flesh) and made us all little clones, each having an identical vision. But He did not do that.

Instead He shared His vision with us, and then nailed His flesh to the cross.

In everything He did (and does) He helped people grow towards their own unique purpose.

Henceforth He considers us as the many different parts, which by working together, become the body of Christ.

Now that is God's heart for ministry!

Reflection and Discussion

1. What is your passion?

2. How can your passion also be your ministry?

3. Who are the beneficiaries of your ministry?

4. What will determine whether or not your ministry is successful?

My Home

Even Levi, who receives tithes, paid tithes through Abraham, so to speak, for he was still in the loins of his father when Melchizedek met him.

Hebrews 7:9-10 (NKJV)

On the night God gave me this message I lay on the sofa quietly suffering. It was the toughest season of my life. I struggled for every breath, but I was not alone—my world was suffocating.

As a bi-vocational pastor, I had been off my regular job because of illness for almost a year. On Sundays it took every ounce of strength just to go to church. Once back home I collapsed on the sofa which is almost literally where I remained until the next Sunday.

That night, the Lord asked me, "Who sinned in the Garden?" When I understood the question, it made me realize that I was failing at some of my responsibilities.

It was suddenly and painfully clear that our inability to have children had nothing to do with Cozzette. It was an outward manifestation of my own broken theology regarding what it means to be a man.

My way was no longer working, and that night God was showing me *His way.*

As I began to understand what God was saying to me, I repented.

Renewed Promise

I had little income to speak of, save a small love offering that the congregation raised once a month.

Prior to that night, Cozzette and I knew that we needed some medical procedures in order to have children. The procedures we needed were very expensive. Because I was raised to believe that people are *only* responsible for themselves and that men and women are equal, I made it Cozzette's job to save the money to have the children, because that's what *she* wanted.

It was going to take one miracle to raise the $13,000 we needed for Cozzette's dream of having children. But then there was this diagnosis, and I needed another miracle just to live.

With that looming diagnosis my logical mind whispered that all hope was lost, that even if we were successful and had children, I would not be around long enough to raise them.

After repenting that night for putting the burden squarely on Cozzette, I told the Lord that I was taking back my responsibilities. I told Him that I would take whatever monies the church raised for me and use it to open a bank account. I promised God that night that I would do whatever it took for Cozzette and I to have children together, even if I had to die in the process.

The following Monday I took my $65 honorarium, and started a savings account dedicated to *Cozzette's* vision.

Though I was incredibly sick and unable to work, even though I was never able to save much money before, *miraculously* the Lord added to that account.

Right in the middle of that tough time, once I got in alignment with God, it seemed as though out of nowhere money that I did not even know was owed to me came looking for me. One former employer sent a letter advising me that he had been looking for me for over ten years. It included a check for $10,000.

Within three months we had all the monies we needed for our first attempt at having children.

That attempt was unsuccessful, yet within a few months we were ready to try again. Nine months later Joseph was born.

Joseph was nearly a year old when I looked at him in Cozzette's arms and realized he needed a brother. "You want to try again?" I asked Cozzette. Jonathan was born about a year later.

By His grace, God delivered me at once from the jaws of death and the brink of barrenness.

After I got it, after there was no doubt that the Lord had given me this message about manhood, He said, "Write it."

With that I knew there was an urgency. That this message was not just for me, but that this was a message He wanted all men to have.

I continue on today, writing, preaching, and sharing His message to men everywhere.

His Way

And so it is written, 'The first man Adam became a living being. The last Adam became a life-giving spirit."

1 Corinthians 15:45 (NKJV)

In our opening pages we asked you to consider the age-old question, "Who sinned in the garden?" Prayerfully, as you have read, you have refined your thoughts on that subject.

Why is the Garden-question important?

Every marksman knows that if there is a great distance between him and his target, a single degree makes all the difference.
The Garden-account is the cradle of our theology. The events that happened there changed the course of our world.

If you cannot draw a straight line between Adam and Jesus, your theology will be off course. The better you understand *how* Adam missed the mark, the better you will stay on target.

Adam's failure was the greatest failure of all time. Had Adam not sinned, Jesus would not have had to come.

If a man does not understand what Adam's sin was and how it tainted the human bloodline, then he will not properly understand why Jesus needed be born of a virgin woman, and he will not grasp why Jesus could not have an earthly father.

Because He was not a tainted male descendant of Adam, Jesus was able to deal with the Garden-problem, rectify Adam's failures, and offer salvation to anyone willing to believe in Him.

Knowing *that* Jesus came, without solidly understanding *why* He needed to come the way He did, is missing something. And, what is missing affects us in a way that impacts His promise *in* us.

Many of us unknowingly have a dual theology. We understand faith when it comes to what Jesus did for us (and rightly so). But, when it comes to rest of the Garden, when it comes to the rest of our world; what we know and understand about Jesus sometimes changes.

If we are not clear about what happened in the Garden, then we make the same mistakes Adam did.

To better understand how people view the Garden-problem, I have posed the following question across the country, and asked both men and women to choose the right answer:

Question: What condemned mankind was Adam's:
- a) Failure to control his wife
- b) Failure to protect the garden
- c) Blaming his wife
- d) Failure to control himself

When asked, more than any other response, men answered that Adam's failure was that he did not control his wife, while more women felt Adam's sin was in failing to protect the garden.

Not Just Physical

In his observation of the physical world Sir Isaac Newton concluded, "For every action there is an equal and opposite reaction." Considering that the physical world is an *image* of the spiritual, there are spiritual applications of this principle.

The most significant action in history (Adam's sin) warranted a *reaction* from our Creator. Jesus' ministry offsets Adam's failure, and shows us *the right way.*

The Control Theory

As I mentioned, more men chose the "control his wife" answer than any other. The next largest group of men considered that control was at least *one* of the factors.

So I ask you, if your wife has her mind made up, can you, or should you try to control her?

Men often feel "control" is where Adam blew it. They further reason that if we could just control our wives today, the world would be better. If this were true, if this was where Adam's failure was, then Jesus' ministry would have been about teaching us how to control our wives. Is that what Jesus came to do? Do you see control in His ministry *at all?*

Which one of you knows a man who completely controls His wife? What does that look like? Can you even remotely see God in that?

In fact, when it comes to the control theory, one can argue that Jesus handles His bride (the church) the same way Adam did—He lets us choose for ourselves.

To the one who is *subject to it,* control is bondage. Jesus did not come to bring us into bondage, but to make us free. That is true for all of us.

If you are a control theorist, then somewhere your theology is failing to make people free. If that is happening, you are not free yourself.

Like Adam, when it is all said and done, the only one we really have control over, is ourselves.

Coming Into Focus

We all have our way of doing things. We all have a sense of fairness. We all have some thoughts about what right and wrong are. If we are really honest, we know that *our way,* our sense of fairness, our righteousness leaves a lot to be desired.

Prayerfully, you have read this far, and while in these pages you have laughed, you have hoped, you have reflected, and more importantly, you have identified areas of your life which you hope to improve.

Prayerfully, you have learned to stop and think, to spend time alone with God, to pray and ask for directions, to let Him influence you above everyone else, to draw your strength from Him, and to seek His heart.

God alone has all the answers. He alone is *completely* righteous. He wants to hear from you. He wants you to hear *Him.*

David is called "a man after God's own heart," not because of his own cleverness, but because he wanted to genuinely hear from God – Regardless of the circumstance.

On the other hand, men like Adam, Cain, King Saul, King Ahab, and Judas Iscariot (who also betrayed Jesus), give us examples of what *not to do.* If there is a common thread that connects these men, it is that they failed to accept the responsibilities God gave *them.* These men caused their own problems, and then blamed their world for their failures.

"That woman You gave me," said Adam. "Am I my brother's keeper?" Asked Cain.

King Saul sought popularity above the word of God, choosing to be responsible *to* the people, instead of being responsible *for* them.

And, Ahab traded his godly responsibilities for the affection of his wife.

Then there was Judas Iscariot, who could not control his vanity and greed; who stole from the money box. And who, for thirty pieces of silver, betrayed our Lord with a kiss.

We could go on and on. From cover to cover we have examples in the Bible of men who sealed their fate when they refused to accept their God-given responsibilities.

On the other hand we see that blessings come wherever a man *takes responsibility.*

That is how David became a man after God's heart. Trusting in the stone that the builders rejected, David slew the giant. David did not run from responsibility, he ran *to* it.

Think about it. He could have said, "It is not my problem." When a volunteer was needed to fight Goliath, he could have gone to the back of the line.

But David sought God's heart. And, because he did, life came to both him *and* his world.

He was not just looking out for himself. David went on to build an entire kingdom where God's people could live and prosper in hope.

I Need You, You Need Me

David did not take his people for granted, nor did he try to do everything himself. He enlisted the help of God's prophet. He was careful to make sure the people that were part of his world were given a chance to do what God called *them to do.*

All those chosen as gatekeepers were two hundred and twelve.
They were recorded by their genealogy, in their villages. David
and Samuel the seer had appointed them to their trusted office.

1 Chr 9:22

"Trusted office" is the single Hebrew word *emunah*. The New American Standard Hebrew and Greek Dictionaries define *emunah* as:

Firmness
Steadfastness
Fidelity
Faith
Faithful
Faithfully
Faithfulness
Honestly
Responsibility
Stability
Steady
Trust
And Truth

These are our job requirements as men and as trustees of God. A "trustee," must be faithful, honest, fully responsible for all that is entrusted to his care. He cannot be wishy-washy, he has to be *trustworthy*. He cannot waver, and he must always be truthful.

We are *gatekeepers* of the life God entrusted to us. That includes lives that come *through* us.

Bringing it Home

If you are thinking you can dismiss this as a small thing, I invite you to consider that David's example is only one man's example. With all we can learn from David, we have an even better example - Jesus.

While showing us what true masculinity looks like, He did not defend Himself. He did not say, "That church You gave me..." He did not fight to have His way.

> *He was oppressed and He was afflicted, yet He opened not His mouth; He was led as a lamb to the slaughter, and as a sheep before its shearers is silent, so He opened not His mouth.*
>
> Isa 53:7

He was spat on, ridiculed, beaten, and nailed to a cross. He endured it all, for your sake and for my sake.

> *Surely He has borne our griefs and carried our sorrows; yet we esteemed Him stricken, smitten by God, and afflicted. But He was wounded for our transgressions, He was bruised for our iniquities; the chastisement for our peace was upon Him, and by His stripes we are healed.*
>
> Isa 53:4-5

> *When they had twisted a crown of thorns, they put it on His head, and a reed in His right hand. And they bowed the knee before Him and mocked Him, saying, "Hail, King of the Jews!" Then they spat on Him, and took the reed and struck Him on the head.*
>
> Mat 27:29-30

Jesus gave us a clear example.

He paid the ultimate price.

God came to this Earth in the form of a man.

He did not come to condemn His world. He came to save it.

He was not the One who sinned, He had done nothing wrong.

God Himself gave every one of us an example of manhood.

Here is His example:

To His last breath Jesus was God, stretching out His arms, allowing Himself to be nailed to a cross, to take responsibility for His world.

And, in so doing, He gave resurrection life to Himself, resurrection life to His world, and purchased redemption for His bride (the church).

I pray that you have found this book and this ministry rewarding. In the next volume we will share practical ways for men to strengthen their Christian walk.

May God bless you and cause you to be everything He made you to be. Amen.

If you would like Pastor Barry to speak at your church, conference, or men's ministry, or, if you would like information about discounts for bulk book purchases, please visit http://www.BarryJenkins.org

Other Fine Books From Barry Jenkins

Do you know for sure that you are living the life you were born to live, and that you are doing what you were meant to do?

Deep down inside, do you have a sense that your destiny is out there waiting for you?

"On the Road to Glory" looks at these questions, through the life of one man from an unlikely place.

Whether you have found your true purpose or are still trying to find it, this book will encourage and inspire you.

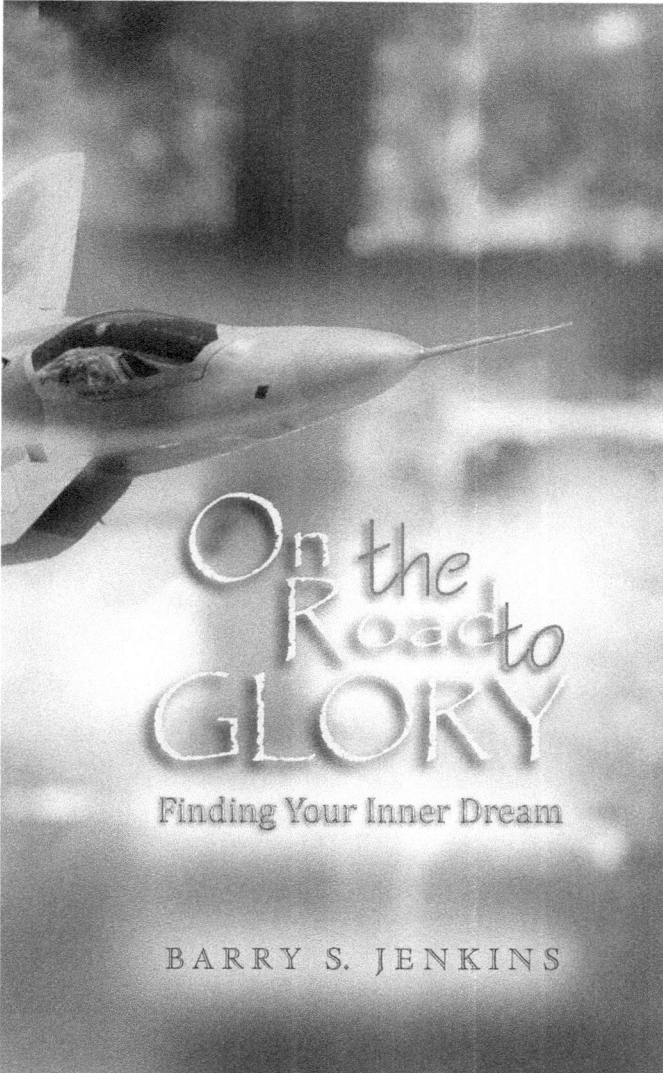

On the Road to
GLORY

Finding Your Inner Dream

BARRY S. JENKINS

www.ingramcontent.com/pod-product-compliance
Lightning Source LLC
Chambersburg PA
CBHW062219080426
42734CB00010B/1954